Natural Rights, the Common Good, and the American Revolution

This book is the fourth in a series in AEI's
"We Hold These Truths: America at 250" initiative.

WE HOLD THESE TRUTHS: AMERICA AT 250

Democracy and the American Revolution

Capitalism and the American Revolution

Religion and the American Revolution

*Natural Rights, the Common Good,
and the American Revolution*

Natural Rights, the Common Good, and the American Revolution

Edited by Yuval Levin,
Adam J. White, and John Yoo

AEI PRESS

Publisher for the American Enterprise Institute
WASHINGTON, DC

ISBN-13: 978-0-8447-5091-0 (Paperback)

Library of Congress Cataloging in Publication data have been applied for.

© 2025 by the American Enterprise Institute for Public Policy Research. All rights reserved. No part of this publication may be used or reproduced in any manner whatsoever without permission in writing from the American Enterprise Institute except in the case of brief quotations embodied in news articles, critical articles, or reviews. The views expressed in the publications of the American Enterprise Institute are those of the authors and do not necessarily reflect the views of the staff, advisory panels, officers, or trustees of AEI.

AEI PRESS

Publisher for the American Enterprise Institute
for Public Policy Research
1789 Massachusetts Avenue, NW
Washington, DC 20036
www.aei.org

Printed in the United States of America

Contents

Introduction 1
Yuval Levin

1. Natural Rights, Culture, and the Common Good 5
   Robert P. George

2. Editing the Declaration 19
   Charles R. Kesler

3. Equality, Liberty, and Rights in the Declaration of Independence 43
   Michael Zuckert

4. How the Declaration Disagrees with John Locke 63
   Daniel E. Burns

5. Humility, Hubris, and the Pursuit of Happiness 93
   Janice Rogers Brown

About the Authors 109

About the Editors 110

Introduction

YUVAL LEVIN

July 4, 2026, will mark the 250th anniversary of the Declaration of Independence and, therefore, of the United States of America. Much was new about the American republic when the founders launched it. Theirs was among the first successful colonial revolts in the known history of the world. It created the first modern democracy and modeled a new form of liberal republicanism that had barely been theorized, let alone enacted before. But the founding was also distinct, and the nation it brought forth has been, too, for its rootedness in a particular philosophy of society and ultimately of the human person.

The Declaration of Independence was a political statement, and the founding was a political act, but both were therefore also inextricably connected to a set of philosophical principles. And in declaring those ideas, the founders of the United States also declared them to be rooted in a conception of nature. "The Laws of Nature and of Nature's God entitle" the nations of the world to assume separate and equal stations among one another. Those laws, in turn, point to a set of propositions about the character of politics and of society. The Declaration states these compactly and powerfully in its famous second paragraph:

> We hold these truths to be self-evident, that all men are created equal, that they are endowed by their Creator with certain unalienable Rights, that among these are Life, Liberty and the pursuit of Happiness.—That to secure these rights, Governments are instituted among Men, deriving their just powers from the consent of the governed,—That whenever any Form

of Government becomes destructive of these ends, it is the Right of the People to alter or to abolish it, and to institute new Government, laying its foundation on such principles and organizing its powers in such form, as to them shall seem most likely to effect their Safety and Happiness.

This declaration of principles invites a host of questions. Just what is the connection between these truths and the right by which nature and God are said to entitle nations to independence? And just what is their connection, in turn, to the relations of individual citizens and their societies? The rights with which all men are said to be endowed seem at first glance like purely individual rights, yet the Declaration of Independence speaks on behalf of a nation and asserts that each nation derives its right to its place in the world from some natural and divine source. Nations are said to be equal just as individuals are. What connects these two bearers of rights—the individual and the community—and which is prior and preeminent?

These questions and countless related ones have given form to the politics of the United States since the founding, and they were of course crucial to what brought about the founding to begin with. They are essential to better understanding the character of our society, yet they remain perplexing and demanding.

Better understanding the character of our society is precisely the purpose of the American Enterprise Institute's "We Hold These Truths: America at 250" initiative, an ambitious celebration of the founding, of which this volume forms a part. Over several years leading up to the anniversary of the Declaration of Independence, we are inviting scholars both within AEI and from other institutions to take up a series of themes important to understanding the American Revolution. These scholars represent a variety of fields and viewpoints, so they will approach each of these themes from various angles. The papers they produce will be published in a series of edited volumes intended to help Americans think more deeply and clearly about our nation's origins, character, and prospects.

Natural Rights, the Common Good, and the American Revolution is the fourth of those books. Its chapters began as papers presented at an AEI conference held in Washington, DC, on December 2, 2024. Other volumes in the series consider the American Revolution in relation to other themes, such as democracy, religion, the legacy of slavery, and the Constitution. In each case, our goal is to help reintroduce readers to their nation's history, thereby enabling them to maturely appreciate the reasons for celebrating the extraordinary milestone of its 250th anniversary.

In the chapters that follow, five eminent scholars of history, philosophy, law, and government consider how we ought to understand the place of natural rights and the meaning of the common good in the American Revolution and the life of the nation it produced.

Robert P. George lays out the natural law foundations of the arguments advanced in the Declaration and sketches the ideal of the common good that emerges from considering the founding in their light.

Charles R. Kesler examines the ways in which the text of the Declaration of Independence was altered by its assorted congressional editors and shows how these changes highlight the Declaration's classical character and purpose.

Michael Zuckert details the structure and substance of the argument put forward in the Declaration's immortal second paragraph. He suggests that it marks not only the document's philosophical premises but also its political ambition.

Daniel E. Burns contends that attributing the political philosophy of the Declaration and the founding primarily to John Locke misrepresents both Locke and the founders—and so obscures the genius of American political ideas rather the clarifying it.

And Janice Rogers Brown elucidates the founders' conception of the pursuit of happiness. She explores how our nation has strayed from that conception and so has too often put happiness, properly understood, beyond our reach.

The scope of these arguments helps to show just how foundational the questions surrounding natural rights and the common good are to the

4 NATURAL RIGHTS AND THE COMMON GOOD

American political tradition, and so how essential they are to what we celebrate when we mark the 250th anniversary of our extraordinary nation.

1

Natural Rights, Culture, and the Common Good

ROBERT P. GEORGE

During the first presidential administration of Donald Trump, Secretary of State Mike Pompeo asked me to assist in the creation of a commission to reevaluate the concept of human rights as it functions in United States foreign and diplomatic policy. The promotion of human rights abroad—and the deployment of the United States' soft and hard power in behalf of human rights—has sat at the center of State Department policy for much of the post–World War II era. Our task, to quote the commission's notice of establishment in the *Federal Register*, was twofold: to identify where the department's human rights discourse had "departed from our nation's founding principles of natural law and natural rights" and to propose reforms to recover the historic understanding of human rights.[1]

Given the ideological sympathies of many State Department career employees, I was not surprised when news of the commission's creation was leaked to the hostile press. Critics on the left attacked the very idea of the commission, mostly by repeating the same cynical (and tired, having been refuted many times) notion that a robust and reason-based account of human rights grounded in timeless principles of natural law was nothing more than a pretext for smuggling sectarian, irrational, and blindly dogmatic religious doctrines into American public policy. In *The New Republic*, for example, Alexis Papazoglou wrote that political arguments based on natural law theory are rooted in "theological" sources that "tend to obscure the political agendas of those invoking them," while the LGBTQ magazine *Advocate* published an article titled "Is State Department's 'Natural Law' Effort Code for Homophobia?"[2]

But in his quest to dismiss natural law theory and a natural law account of human rights as medieval religious dogma that should not be taken seriously in the 21st century, Papazoglou made the important observation that

> the wording in the State Department's announcement of this new Commission on Unalienable Rights implies the premise that international human rights have expanded over the years to include rights that would not be recognized under the tradition of natural law and of natural rights embodied in the U.S.'s eighteenth-century founding documents.[3]

Exactly. That overreach—the detachment of human rights from any rigorous philosophical substance or comprehensive vision of human goods and human flourishing, with the accompanying marginalization of the understanding of human rights that the founders endorsed in, above all, the Declaration of Independence—was precisely what the State Department commission was intended to identify and rectify. Its mission was to correct the ideologically motivated redefinition of human rights—or, to use the traditional term that invokes the concept's philosophical origins, natural rights—that viewed rights as rooted in nothing more than ill-defined and highly abstract notions of autonomy, self-determination, self-authorship, and the ability to fulfill one's desires (whether those desires are rational and morally defensible or not).

Rights, according to this view, are not derived from any substantive conception of human goods and human flourishing—even for those who claim to eschew moral relativism, one can have the "human right" to do something morally wrong precisely as one has the right to do something virtuous or morally upright. Rights are simply the person's entitlement to freely pursue desires, feelings, and passions, without any requirements or responsibilities (whether legally enforceable or not) beyond the duty to avoid violating the rights of others. One's right to freedom from coercion in matters of religion, for example, is not a correlative of a moral obligation to pursue the truth about the most important existential and transcendental questions and act in accord with one's best judgments of the truth; instead, the right to religious freedom is rooted in a person's claim to believe what they want, so long as they don't impose their beliefs on others.

In this framework, the freedom—the right—is treated as something substantively good and morally desirable for its own sake, whose only limits appear when one's desires clash with others' ability to exercise their autonomy to pursue and fulfill their own desires. (Consider, for example, the revisionist view of sexual morality that the only legitimate moral metric to evaluate a sexual act is whether both or all parties consent to it.) The idea of right is detached from the good—"prior to that of the good," in the famous phrase of the liberal political philosopher John Rawls[4]—and, at times, set directly against the good.

Still, the descriptive fact that the *New Republic* article acknowledged is an important one: The authors of our nation's founding documents—especially the Declaration of Independence, with its emphatic pronouncement that our "unalienable Rights" to "Life, Liberty and the pursuit of Happiness" constitute self-evident moral realities that demand, as a matter of justice and political morality, state recognition and protection—understood natural rights to be substantively grounded in the goods they protect. The pursuit of happiness, for the founders, was not a matter of fulfilling one's subjective desires—whatever they happened to be—as if happiness were merely a pleasant psychological state (one that might, just as well, be produced by Prozac or other drugs). On the contrary, the concept of happiness was for the American founders morally inflected—something akin to flourishing or fulfillment, rather than to a pleasant psychological state. Contemporary progressives, while they seek to jettison this understanding as a relic of the past and replace it with a doctrine that celebrates personal autonomy and expressive individualism, do right by at least being honest about how our forefathers conceived fundamental rights.

Political Authority, the Common Good, and the Pursuit of Happiness

Grasping these distinct ideas of happiness can direct us to the relationship between governments' moral duty to protect the pursuit of happiness and the natural law account of goods and rights. Here, I think we ought to consider the pursuit of happiness (again, as the founders understood the term) in light of a particular understanding of political authority and the nature of the common good, which any ruler has a moral duty to uphold and serve.[5]

If we understand the concept of the common good properly—and I will say a word about that in a moment—then we will see that no decision by political authority that violates a requirement of justice (and respect for human rights is a requirement of justice) is truly for the common good, and no decision that genuinely upholds and serves the common good will fail to advance the cause of justice.

The common good requires officials who are charged to make laws, execute them, and resolve disputes under them. To grasp this is to begin to see the sense in which public officials are what we call "public servants." Members of societies face a range—sometimes a vast one—of challenges and opportunities requiring both means-to-ends and persons-to-persons coordination, including, in the case of complex societies, coordination problems presented by the large number and complexity of other coordination problems. Since such problems cannot, as a practical matter, be addressed and resolved by unanimity, *authority*—political authority—is required.[6] Institutions have to be created and maintained, and persons need to be installed in these institutions' offices to make the decisions that must be made and do the things that must be done, for the sake of protecting public health, safety, and morals; upholding the rights and dignity of individuals, families, and nongovernmental entities of various descriptions; and advancing the common good.

This would be true even in a society of perfect saints, where no one ever sought more than his fair share from the common stock, violated the rights of others, or deliberately acted contrary to the common good. Even in such a society, effective coordination for the sake of common goals—and, thus, for the good of all—would be required, and seeking unanimity, assuming a large and fairly complex society, would not be practical.[7] So authority would be required, which means persons exercising authority would be required.

But the moral justification for officials holding and exercising power is service to the good of all, the common good. And the common good is not an abstraction or Platonic form hovering somewhere beyond the concrete well-being—the flourishing—of the flesh-and-blood persons constituting the community. It *is* the well-being of those persons, families, and other associations of persons—Edmund Burke's "little platoon[s]" of civil society[8]—of which they are members.

The right of public officials to exercise power is rooted in their duty to exercise their authority in the interest of all—in other words, the basis of the *right* to rule is the *duty* to serve. And the realities that constitute service are the various elements of the common good. By doing what is for the common good—and by avoiding doing anything that harms it—rulers fulfill their obligations to the people over whom they exercise authority. They thus serve the people's interests, welfare, and flourishing—in a word, *them*.

I don't know how to improve on the definition of the common good proposed by John Finnis in his magisterial book *Natural Law and Natural Rights*. The common good, he says, is

> a set of conditions which enables the members of a community to attain *for themselves* reasonable objectives, or to realize reasonably *for themselves* the value(s), for the sake of which they have reason to collaborate with each other (positively and/or negatively) in a community.[9] (Emphasis added.)

Now, every community—from the basic community of a family to a church or other community of religious faith, a mutual aid society or other civic association, and a business firm—has a common good. The common good of some communities is fundamentally an intrinsic rather than an instrumental good. That is true, for example, of the community of the family or, in Christian and Jewish traditions, communities of faith.

The common good is, in this sense, facilitative. Its elements are what enable people to do things, individually and in cooperation, that significantly constitute their all-around, or integral, flourishing. Under favoring conditions, people can more fully and successfully carry out reasonable projects, pursue reasonable objectives, and, thus, participate in values—including some values that are inherently social, in that they fulfill persons' capacities for noninstrumental forms of interpersonal communion—which indeed constitute their well-being and fulfillment.

Properly understood, then, the common good requires, as a matter of justice, limited government—government that respects the needs and rights of people to pursue objectives and realize goods *for themselves*. The fundamental role of legitimate government, and thus the responsibility of legitimate rulers—rulers who serve—is not to do things for people that they could do for themselves; it is, rather, to help establish and maintain conditions that favor people's doing things for themselves and with and for each other. Governments should do things *for people* (as opposed to letting them do things *for themselves*) only when individuals and the nongovernmental institutions of civil society cannot be reasonably expected to do them for themselves. Finnis used the word "enables," and it is the right word here: Government's legitimate concern is with the establishment and maintenance of the *conditions* under which members of the community are *enabled* to pursue the projects and goals by and through which they participate in the goods constitutive of their flourishing.

Now, what about the common good of the political community—which good rulers serve (and to which citizens also have responsibilities)? Is it fundamentally an intrinsic good or an instrumental good? There is, in what Sir Isaiah Berlin referred to as the central tradition of Western thought about morality (including political morality), a powerful current of belief that the common good of political society is an intrinsic good.[10]

This seems clearly to have been the view of Aristotle, and many Thomists of the strict scholastic persuasion are convinced that it was the view of Aristotle's greatest interpreter and expositor, Thomas Aquinas.

Finnis, however, argues that the common good of political society is nevertheless fundamentally an instrumental, not an intrinsic, good.[11] He further argues that the instrumental nature of the common good of political society entails limitations on the legitimate scope of governmental authority—limitations that, though not in every case easily articulable in the language of rights, are requirements of justice. Although I differ, at the margins, from Professor Finnis (who, along with Joseph Raz, was my graduate supervisor in Oxford) on the question of just what the limits are (and in particular whether they exclude moral paternalism in principle), I agree that the common good of political society is fundamentally an instrumental good and that this entails moral limits on justified governmental power.[12]

If we understand the common good—if we have a grasp of what constitutes or conduces to human flourishing and what does not—we will recognize that limited government is important also because it permits the functioning and flourishing of nongovernmental institutions of civil society. Those little platoons of the family, the church, and so forth perform society's most essential health, education, and welfare functions better than government ever conceivably could. They play the primary role in transmitting to each new generation the virtues without which free societies cannot survive—basic honesty, integrity, self-restraint, concern for others, respect for others' dignity and rights, civic-mindedness, and the like.[13]

These nongovernmental authority structures represent a crucial way power is properly diffused rather than concentrated in the hands of the state and its officials. They can play their role only when government is limited—for unlimited government always usurps their authority and destroys their autonomy, usually recruiting or commandeering them into being state functionary organs. And where they play their proper role, they help create conditions in which the ideal of limited government is much more likely to be realized and preserved and its benefits enjoyed by the people.

I think we ought to understand the right to the pursuit of happiness proclaimed in the Declaration of Independence in light of the nature of the political common good that I've outlined here—in which sufficient conditions of justice, freedom, and public morality facilitate citizens' reasoned pursuit of human goods and flourishing. Our forefathers highly esteemed freedom—which they understood as oriented toward authentic human goods and valuable only when exercised morally in furtherance of those goods. In their rejection of the tyrannies of the British Crown, liberty and the pursuit of happiness constituted goods worth fighting a revolution to defend.

Still, liberty and—even more obviously—the pursuit of happiness, like the common good of political society, do not constitute ultimate ends of human action in the same way that intrinsically desirable goods such as life, intellectual knowledge, friendship, marriage, the family, beauty, and religion do. Liberty and the pursuit of happiness are not valuable for their own sakes—they are valuable only when exercised instrumentally in service of other goods. Indeed, the word "pursuit" necessarily implies its conditional nature—if a person failed in their pursuit of a good (perhaps even by directly acting against it), they would not have realized any good by their failed attempt.

The authors of the Declaration viewed the failure of the British authorities to uphold conditions of the common good—equal justice, the rule of law, and just limits on governmental coercion, for example—as morally sufficient reasons to seek the colonies' independence from what they considered a corrupted political authority. They listed specific ways the king's unjust actions had damaged the common good: He had refused his assent to laws passed by colonial legislatures, sought to control judges and influence the administration of justice, and curtailed civil liberties without the consent of the colonists' representatives, for example. He had breached the moral limits of both his office and justified governmental power. In essence, the founders' argument was that the king and his agents had, through "abuses and usurpations" of political authority, gravely damaged the common good of the political community—thus impeding the ability of citizens to engage in the pursuit of human goods and flourishing (happiness).

Political Culture and Civic Virtue

The concepts of duty and obligation noted above—which, once again, are inextricably intertwined with the rights and freedoms proclaimed in the Declaration of Independence—bring me to the critical, yet oddly neglected, subject of political culture and civic virtue.

In 2008, the celebrated legal philosopher Jeremy Waldron visited his native New Zealand to read his countrymen the riot act about what he condemned as the abysmal quality of that nation's parliamentary debate. The bulk of his lecture was devoted to an analysis and critique of a range of factors leading to the impoverishment of legislative deliberation, warranting the stinging title he assigned to his lecture: "Parliamentary Recklessness." Its penultimate section, titled "Parliamentary Debate," delivered a thoroughly gloomy appraisal.

But instead of ending there and offering no grounds for hope, Waldron concluded with a section titled "The Quality of Public Debate," in which he pointed to the possibility that the deficiencies of parliamentary debate might be at least partially compensated for by a higher quality of *public* debate, even hinting that this could prompt the reforms necessary to at least begin restoring the integrity of parliamentary debate. But he warned that things could also go the other way. The corruption of parliamentary debate could infect "the political culture at large," driving public debate down to the condition of parliamentary debate.

So, in a sense, it is up to the people to decide whether they will rise above the corruption that has demeaned parliamentary politics or permit it to "infect the political culture at large."[14] But "the people" are not some undifferentiated mass; they are people, you and me, individuals.

Of course, considered as isolated actors there is not a lot that individuals can do to affect the political culture. But individuals can cooperate for greater effectiveness in prosecuting an agenda of conservation or reform, and they can create associations and institutions that are capable of making a difference—advocacy groups, think tanks, and the like.

A critical element in any discussion of the quality of democratic deliberation and decision-making is the indispensable role that the nongovernmental institutions of civil society—those little platoons, yet again—play in sustaining a culture in which political institutions do what they are established to do, do it well, and stay within their limits. And so we must be mindful that bad behavior by political institutions—which means bad behavior by the people who exercise power as holders of public offices—can weaken, enervate, and even corrupt these institutions of civil society, rendering them for all intents and purposes impotent to resist the bad behavior and useless to the cause of political reform.

This is true generally, and it is certainly true with respect to the bad behavior of public officials who betray their obligations to serve by transgressing the bounds of their constitutional authority and the limits embodied in the doctrine of subsidiarity. Constitutional structural constraints are important, but they are effective only where they are effectually supported by the people—that is, by the political culture. The people need to understand and value them—enough to resist usurpations by their rulers even when unconstitutional programs offer immediate gratifications or relief from urgent problems. This, in turn, requires certain virtues—strengths of character—among the people. But these virtues do not just fall down on people from the heavens. They have to be transmitted through the generations and nurtured by each generation.

James Madison said that "a well-instructed people alone can be permanently a free people."[15] And that is true. It points to the fact that even the best constitutional structures, even the strongest structural constraints on governmental power, aren't worth the paper they are printed on if people do not understand them, value them, and have the will to resist the blandishments of those offering something tempting in return for giving them up or letting them be violated without swift and certain political retaliation.

But it is also true that virtue is needed, and that's not merely a matter of improving civics teaching in homes and schools. In *Federalist* 51, Madison famously defended the Constitution of the United States as "supplying by opposite and rival interests, the defect of better motives." He made this point immediately after observing that the first task of government is to control the governed, and the second is to control itself. He allowed that "a dependence on the people is no doubt the primary controul on the government; but experience has taught mankind the necessity of auxiliary precautions"—hence the constitutional structural constraints, among other things. But even in this formulation, they do not stand alone; indeed, they are presented as secondary. What is also necessary—indeed, primary—is a healthy and vibrant political culture, "a dependence on the people" to keep the rulers in line.[16]

That brings us back to the role and importance of virtue. John Adams understood as well as anyone the general theory of the Constitution. He was the ablest scholar and political theorist of the founding generation. He certainly got the point about "supplying . . . the defect of better motives," yet he also understood that the health of the political culture was an indispensable element of the success of the constitutional enterprise—an enterprise of ensuring that the rulers stay within the bounds of their legitimate authority and indeed be servants of the common good, servants of the people they rule.

Adams remarked that "our Constitution is made only for a moral and religious People. It is wholly inadequate to the government of any other."[17] Why? Because a people lacking in virtue could be counted on to trade liberty for protection, financial or personal security, comfort, being taken care of, or having their problems solved quickly. And there will always be people occupying or standing for public office who are happy to offer that deal—in return for an expansion of their power.

So the question is how to form people fitted out with the virtues that make them worthy of freedom and capable of preserving constitutionally limited government, even in the face of strong and inevitable temptations to compromise it away. Here we see the central political role and significance of the most basic institutions of civil society—the family, the religious community, private organizations of all types that are devoted to the inculcation of knowledge and morals, private (often religious) educational institutions, and the like, which are in the business of transmitting essential virtues. These are, as is often said, mediating institutions that provide a buffer between the individual and the power of the central state.

It is ultimately the autonomy, integrity, and general flourishing of these institutions that will determine the fate of limited constitutional government. This is not only because of their primary and indispensable role in transmitting virtues; it is also because their performance of health, education, and welfare functions is the only real alternative to removing these functions to larger and higher associations—that is, to government. When government expands to play the primary role in performing these functions, the ideal of limited government is soon lost, no matter the formal structural constraints of the Constitution. And the corresponding weakening of these institutions' status and authority damages their ability to perform all their functions, including their moral and pedagogical ones. With that, they surely lose their capacity to influence for good the political culture, which, in the end, is the whole shooting match when it comes to whether the ruler can truly be a servant.

Pursuing Happiness Properly

At the foundation of America's greatness are the virtues of its people. Those virtues are what sustain the principles and practices of constitutional government. But it is not, or not primarily, those principles and practices that impart the virtues on which they depend. It is first and foremost the little platoons—above all, the family.

Do you want to make America great? Good. That's what we should all want. But in recent decades, the American family has suffered massive disintegration, which has devastated the poorest and most vulnerable sectors of our society. That disintegration has weakened us morally and spiritually. All the material wealth and military power in the world cannot make up for it. So let us make no mistake: American greatness will not be restored without the restoration of strong and healthy families—marriage-based families. American greatness ultimately depends on the greatness of American families, for they alone can transmit the virtues on which all else depends.

I will conclude by underscoring that when we recognize the common good of political society—the conditions that best facilitate the pursuit of happiness among the citizenry—as properly instrumental, the other pieces fall into place. When we properly characterize that end toward which political action is legitimately directed, then the nature of rights, the necessity of duty and obligation in any discussion of rights, the need of a political culture in which civic virtue is encouraged and rewarded, and the purpose of freedom can all be more easily understood. We should be grateful that our forefathers provided us with the seeds of such wisdom in the Declaration of Independence and other documents of the founding era.

Notes

1. US Department of State, "Notice of Intent to Establish an Advisory Committee," *Federal Register* 84, no. 104 (May 30, 2019): 25109, https://www.federalregister.gov/documents/2019/05/30/2019-11300/department-of-state-commission-on-unalienable-rights.

2. Alexis Papazoglou, "The Sneaky Politics of 'Natural Law,'" *The New Republic*, June 13, 2009, https://newrepublic.com/article/154192/sneaky-politics-natural-law; and Trudy Ring, "Is State Department's 'Natural Law' Effort Code for Homophobia?," *Advocate*, June 1, 2019, https://www.advocate.com/politics/2019/6/01/state-departments-natural-law-effort-code-homophobia.

3. Papazoglou, "The Sneaky Politics of 'Natural Law.'"

4. John Rawls, *A Theory of Justice* (Harvard University Press, 1971), 31, 396.

5. This section and the following one draw from Robert P. George, *Constitutional Structures and Civic Virtues*, Baltimore Bar Library, http://www.barlib.org/Constitutional%20Structures%20and%20Civic%20Virtues.pdf.

6. On the rational (and moral) basis of political authority, see generally John Finnis, *Natural Law and Natural Rights*, 2nd ed. (Oxford University Press, 2011), 231–59.

7. See John Finnis, "Law as Co-Ordination," *Ratio Juris* 2, no. 1 (1989): 97–104, https://onlinelibrary.wiley.com/doi/10.1111/j.1467-9337.1989.tb00029.x.

8. Edmund Burke, "Reflections on the Revolution in France," in *The Works of the Right Honourable Edmund Burke*, vol. 3 (1887; Project Gutenberg, 2005), https://www.gutenberg.org/files/15679/15679-h/15679-h.htm#REFLECTIONS.

9. Finnis, *Natural Law and Natural Rights*, 155.

10. Isaiah Berlin, *The Crooked Timber of Humanity: Chapters in the History of Ideas* (Alfred A. Knopf, 1991), 208.

11. John Finnis, "Is Natural Law Theory Compatible with Limited Government?," in Robert P. George, ed., *Natural Law, Liberalism, and Morality: Contemporary Essays* (Clarendon Press, 1996), 1–26 (esp. at 5–9).

12. Robert P. George, "The Concept of Public Morality," *The American Journal of Jurisprudence* 45, no. 1 (2000): 17–31, https://academic.oup.com/ajj/article-abstract/45/1/17/218013.

13. See Peter L. Berger and Richard John Neuhaus, *To Empower People: The Role of Mediating Structures in Public Policy* (American Enterprise Institute, 1977), https://www.aei.org/wp-content/uploads/2023/07/AEI-STUDIES-POLITICAL-139-1.pdf.

14. Jeremy Waldron, "Parliamentary Recklessness: Why We Need to Legislate More Carefully," lecture, Heritage Hotel, Auckland, New Zealand, July 28, 2008, 32–33, https://maxim.org.nz/content/uploads/2021/03/SJGL-2008-Monograph-Jeremy-Waldron.pdf.

15. James Madison, "Second Annual Message to Congress," speech, December 5, 1810, https://millercenter.org/the-presidency/presidential-speeches/december-5-1810-second-annual-message.

16. *Federalist*, no. 51 (James Madison or Alexander Hamilton), https://founders.archives.gov/documents/Hamilton/01-04-02-0199.

17. John Adams to the Officers of the First Brigade of the Third Division of the Militia of Massachusetts, October 11, 1798, Founders Online, https://founders.archives.gov/documents/Adams/99-02-02-3102.

2

Editing the Declaration

CHARLES R. KESLER

Having spent the better part of 25 years editing the *Claremont Review of Books*, I am happy to confess an occupational bias. This would be a better world if we had more and better editors. In their absence, without their authority, book publishing, journalism, politics, and the web have grown anarchical and ugly. The world grows hyper-Protestant—every man his own priest *and editor*, or non-editor. All id and no ego or superego.

Although editors are not perfect, at their best they introduce an element of reflection, circumspection, and regard for the audience and the argument that even the best authors could use from time to time. This is true even of Thomas Jefferson, "Author of the Declaration of American Independence," as he styled himself on his tombstone, one of the three accomplishments he thought worthy of inclusion there. (The other two were author of "the Statute of Virginia for religious freedom" and "Father of the University of Virginia." He discreetly omitted president of the United States, vice president, US secretary of state, governor of Virginia, and other, lesser achievements.)

Properly speaking, however, Jefferson was not author but draftsman of the Declaration, inasmuch as he drafted it as an official paper of, and for, the Second Continental Congress. He refrained from using the definite article and calling himself "the" author because he served as one of five members of the committee appointed by the Congress to produce a declaration of independence, which the Congress edited and then ratified. He didn't call himself its "principal" author, either, presumably because, as Thomas Hobbes wrote, shared honors are diminished. So he left it at the proud but slightly ambiguous or even misleading "Author of the Declaration of American Independence." To be fair, Jefferson was not always so possessive about his authorship. In his famous letter commenting on the subject, he wrote to Henry Lee on May 8, 1825:

> All American Whigs thought alike on these subjects. when forced therefore to resort to arms for redress, an appeal to the tribunal of the world was deemed proper for our justification. this was the object of the Declaration of Independance . . . to place before mankind the common sense of the subject; [in] terms so plain and firm, as to command their assent, and to justify ourselves in the independant stand we were compelled to take. . . . It was intended to be an expression of the american mind, and to give to that expression the proper tone and spirit called for by the occasion. all it's authority rests then on the harmonising sentiments of the day, whether expressed, in conversns in letters, printed essays or in the elementary books of public right, as Aristotle, Cicero, Locke, Sidney Etc.[1]

Fascinating in several respects, that letter traces the Declaration's authority not to Jefferson's role as its author but to "the harmonising sentiments of the day," including the sentiments of at least four authors of "elementary books of public right," and, it seems, common sense, none of them American. Jefferson is the advocate who arranges and pleads the American case before the jury of mankind.

The story of how the Declaration was drafted and edited has been well told—so far as we understand it, for there are still gaps in our knowledge of the process—by Carl Becker in his classic *The Declaration of Independence: A Study on the History of Political Ideas* (1922) and 75 years later by Pauline Maier in her impressive *American Scripture: Making the Declaration of Independence* (1997). But the story does not draw out its own implications. In this chapter, I ponder the significance of Jefferson's draft and the editorial changes to it that yielded the official text—and especially their significance for the understanding of natural rights and the common good in the American Revolution.

Editing by Committee

The Committee of Five, appointed by Congress to draft a declaration of independence, consisted of Jefferson, John Adams, the old and gout-ridden Benjamin Franklin, Roger Sherman of Connecticut, and Robert Livingston of New York. They left no minutes of their meetings; to understand them we must basically gaze backward from later accounts—mostly much later accounts, between 25 and 50 years later, contradictory and incomplete, left by Jefferson and Adams. In his autobiography of 1805, Adams said the Committee of Five deputed a subcommittee of two, Jefferson and him, to prepare a first draft. Adams then persuaded Jefferson that the Virginian should take the lead. In 1823, the 80-year-old Jefferson remembered it differently. The Committee of Five met, he recalled, and "unanimously pressed on myself alone to make the draught." He consented, but before sending his draft to the Committee he sent it separately, Jefferson said, "to Dr. Franklin and Mr. Adams, requesting their corrections, because they were the two members of whose judgments and amendments I wished most to have the benefit. . . . Their alterations were two or three only, and merely verbal."[2]

Perhaps the most improving and memorable changes to Jefferson's initial version were by his own hand. Before sending the draft to Adams, Jefferson changed "We hold these truths to be sacred and undeniable" to "We hold these truths to be self-evident."[3] Self-evident is stronger, shorter, and more specific, connecting to Aristotle's logical writings and to the textbook definition of a self-evident truth (following Aristotle, among others) as one in which the meaning of the predicate is contained in the subject. Every self-evident truth is undeniable, but not everything undeniable (e.g., the conclusion of logical demonstrations) is self-evident. By raising the topic of self-evidence so boldly, Jefferson's revision raises the question of whether all five of the truths discussed in the Declaration's great second paragraph are self-evident. (This is the question pursued in Michael Zuckert's chapter of this book.)

The final two truths might seem to follow from the first three, in which case the final two would not, strictly speaking, be self-evident. The draftsman and the printers of the Declaration took care to link the five truths by beginning each clause with the word "that," as we can see:

> We hold these truths to be self-evident, that all men are created equal, that they are endowed by their Creator with certain unalienable Rights, that among these are Life, Liberty and the pursuit of Happiness.—That to secure these rights, Governments are instituted among Men, deriving their just powers from the consent of the governed,—That whenever any Form of Government becomes destructive of these ends, it is the Right of the People to alter or to abolish it, and to institute new Government, laying its foundation on such principles and organizing its powers in such form, as to them shall seem most likely to effect their Safety and Happiness.

But Jefferson and his coadjutors may have indicated a bit of the ambiguity in the connection between the first three and the last two truths by inserting in the broadside edition, published in Philadelphia by John Dunlap on July 4, a double dash after the word "Happiness," thus separating even as they connected the two sets of truths. Eighteenth-century punctuation, capitalization, and spelling often varied, of course, as a comparison of the committee's drafts would show; and so it is difficult to draw firm conclusions from this evidence.[4]

Subsequently, Jefferson edited the rest of that great sentence, which had initially stated "that all men are created equal and independent, that from that equal creation they derive equal rights, some of which are inherent and inalienable."[5] There were too many "equals" there, and men are better off being "endowed by their Creator with certain unalienable

Rights" than having to derive those rights themselves (presumably) from their equal creation. "Independent" doesn't really add anything to "created equal," and besides, as Becker commented, after "self-evident," the paragraph doesn't need a second word ending in "-dent."[6]

It was the Continental Congress itself, meeting as the Committee of the Whole, that performed the most extensive editorial work on the Committee of Five's draft Declaration. The Congress pored over it for three successive days. Several paragraphs were greatly altered and a few, "fully a quarter of his text," according to Maier, omitted altogether.[7] She judges it one of the most successful exercises in group editing of all time. I would agree. But Jefferson didn't see it that way, decrying the Congress's "depredations" and taking the occasion to record one of the classic stories by and about Franklin, who was sitting near Jefferson in Independence Hall.

Franklin "perceived," Jefferson later recalled, "that I was not insensible" to the Congress's "mutilations" of his and the committee's text. "I have made it a rule," said Franklin,

> whenever in my power, to avoid becoming the draughtsman of papers to be reviewed by a public body. I took my lesson from an incident which I will relate to you. When I was a journeyman printer, one of my companions, an apprentice Hatter, having served out his time, was about to open shop for himself. His first concern was to have a handsome signboard, with a proper inscription. He composed it in these words: "John Thompson, Hatter, makes and sells hats for ready money," with a figure of a hat subjoined. But he thought he would submit it to his friends for their amendments. The first he shewed it to thought the word "hatter" tautologous, because followed by the words "makes hats" which shew he was a hatter. It was struck out. The next observed that the word "makes" might as well be omitted, because his customers would not care who made the hats. If good and to their mind, they would buy, by whomsoever made.

He struck it out. A third said he thought the words "for ready money" were useless as it was not the custom of the place to sell on credit. Every one who purchased expected to pay. They were parted with, and the inscription now stood "John Thompson sells hats." "*Sells* hats" says his next friend? Why nobody will expect you to give them away. What then is the use of that word? It was stricken out, and "hats" followed it, the rather, as there was one painted on the board. So his inscription was reduced ultimately to "John Thompson" with the figure of a hat subjoined.[8]

That's a marvelous Franklin story, suggesting the former printer's appreciation of the ruthless business of editing. At the same time, it was advice to his young friend Jefferson to beware of expecting an author's satisfaction from a draftsman's commission.

And it was also a subtle lesson in self-evidence and the approach or access to truth. It wasn't necessary to advertise that a hatter makes hats for, and sells them to, human beings, rather than for other kinds of animals, nor that one hat per head at a time was both the customary and natural usage. Nor that the image of a hat on the signboard was not meant to advertise the only model of hat Thompson produced and sold; it was clear that the image showed one of an infinite or at any rate very large number of hats of various sizes, colors, patterns, and styles that could be purchased or commissioned therein. One might imagine that, if prompted, Franklin might have advised his young friend that it wasn't necessary to say everything explicitly, to decide questions not yet ripe or relevant, and to call George III a would-be tyrant, for example, twice in the same state paper. Indeed, the Declaration remains silent on a surprising number of themes, never mentioning, for example, the regime types of the states officially themselves made free and independent by this Declaration. The term "republic" never occurs, nor "democracy," nor "commonwealth."

The majority of the Congress's editorial changes to the Declaration concerned the long, central recitation of the charges against George III, attempting to prove he had "in direct object the establishment of an absolute Tyranny over these States" and that "a Prince, whose character is thus marked by every act which may define a Tyrant, is unfit to be a ruler of a free people." It is these "mutilations," including the wholesale striking of his long paragraph on the evils of the slave trade, with which Jefferson was presumably struggling when Franklin noticed his friend's unease. These were the words on the Declaration's signboard that the Committee of the Whole was so blithely expunging. These were the deletions Franklin was endeavoring to reassure the suffering author were not as ruinous as he feared.

One can sympathize with Jefferson's concern. He had arranged the Declaration as a kind of legal and political brief, beginning with a statement of the relevant laws, in this case the "Laws of Nature and of Nature's God"; the Americans' rights and duties under those laws; and the willful injuries against those rights and duties by the king (that long central indictment) and culminating with the injunctive relief the Americans sought from the tribunal of mankind—to sever the political bands linking them to the British Empire and to be recognized as free and independent states, conducting a just war for their independence against the tyrant who intended to oppress them.

Neither the Congress nor the Committee of Five had altered this basic structure of the Declaration's argument as Jefferson had conceived it—even though, as Franklin perhaps indicated gently, they found the argument a little overdone. Although Adams wrote that he liked the "flights of oratory" in Jefferson's draft, including what Adams called "the vehement philippic against Negro slavery," meant as the crescendo of the case against George III, Adams much later (in 1822) admitted

> there were other expressions which I would not have inserted if I had drawn it up, particularly that which called the king tyrant. I thought this too personal; for I never believed George to be a tyrant in disposition and in nature; I always believed him to be deceived by his courtiers on both sides of the Atlantic, and in his official capacity only, cruel. I thought the expression too

passionate, and too much like scolding, for so grave and solemn a document.⁹

Still, Adams not did object either in the Committee of Five or in the Committee of the Whole. Though the king may not have been a natural tyrant, he was acting the part rather convincingly, Adams suggested, so much so that rebellion and independence were *necessary*—there was no other choice.

Thoughts on Government

The Declaration's need to arraign George III's character as tyrannical depended, of course, on the implicit refusal of both the drafting committee and the Second Continental Congress to follow Thomas Paine's argument in *Common Sense*, published in America to great acclaim in January 1776. Paine had excoriated both hereditary monarchy in general and the mixed regime of the British constitution in particular as reactionary, irrational, and evil. For Paine, one didn't need to prove George III a tyrant; it was enough that he was a hereditary monarch, the effectual truth of which was tyranny anyway.

Common Sense attracted hundreds of thousands of readers in America but not one vote in Congress. The Declaration of Independence, therefore, had to prove or illustrate the long train of tyrannical abuses and usurpations of which George III was accused, thus establishing beyond reasonable doubt that at some point he had ceased to be a *king*, nominally or presumptively, seeking the common good of his people, and had on the contrary revealed himself to be a *tyrant*, out to pursue his own good above all else. The rhetorical and logical burden of proof assumed by, and in, the Declaration shows how far apart the Continental Congress's frame of mind stood from Paine's.

That difference would have been emphasized still further had the Committee of Five and the Congress entered another subject already alluded to, which they avoided for the most part—namely, the former colonies', now independent states', need for new constitutions. Starting in the fall of 1775, the Congress had named five members, including Adams and Richard Henry Lee of Virginia, to a committee to reply to an entreaty from New Hampshire asking what the colony should do for a government, now that it had driven out the royal governor. Adams, as the chairman of the committee, offered a resolution "recommending to the provincial convention of New Hampshire" that it "call a full and free representation of the people" to establish a new form of government that in their judgment "will best produce the happiness of the people."[10] In our day, to resort to popular sovereignty may seem like plain common sense, but in 1775, it was a revolutionary suggestion.

By April 1776, Adams had turned his ongoing correspondence into the short pamphlet *Thoughts on Government*, in which he proffered advice on what kind of government the new states should in general adopt. Adams recommended republican government, with a bicameral legislature, a strong executive, an independent judiciary, and separation of powers. To the question why the Declaration itself did not enter into this subject, Adams would have had a good answer—that was another committee's job, the committee consisting of him and Richard Henry Lee.

Adams's suggestions were already *implicit*, and in later iterations would become *explicit*, criticisms of Paine's simpler or more populist brand of republicanism. Paine's cardinal principle, as he put it in *Common Sense*, was "a principle in nature which no art can overturn, viz. that the more simple anything is, the less liable it is to be disordered, and the easier repaired when disordered."[11] By the light of this principle, Britain's complicated regime of mixed government—of constitutional checks and balances among the one, the few, and the many—was profoundly misconceived, a combination of the injustice of monarchy with the folly of hereditary succession. Adams's prescription for complicated republican regimes in the American states, overflowing with checks and balances, struck Paine as a foolish attempt to emulate the corrupt British model. Much better, simpler, and more republican, Paine insisted, would have been unicameral legislatures with weak executives and judiciaries. This was a debate that was only beginning among the Americans, but it represented another fault line that could have begun to move earlier or more joltingly than it did.

By the following month, May 1776, Adams had moved a resolution, which Congress had approved, to recommend to all the remaining colonial administrations that they "adopt such Government as shall in the Opinion of the Representatives of the People best conduce to the happiness and safety of their Constituents in particular and America in general."[12] The Declaration never mentions dissolving government without mentioning at once the need to institute a new form of government, and Adams and Jefferson would become personally involved in those efforts to write new constitutions in their home states—in Jefferson's case, well before the Declaration had been approved by the Congress. The implicit constitutionalism of the Declaration—which can be most strikingly discerned in the indictment of George III's *unconstitutional* actions—was broad enough to countenance Jefferson's and Adams's own somewhat divergent thoughts about republican government, and perhaps even to encompass Paine's and Adams's even more divergent thoughts about the best form of republicanism.

Both the drafting committee and the Congress accepted Jefferson's *other* rhetorical and constitutional presumption in the draft Declaration as well—namely, that the only legitimate connection between the American people and the British Empire ran through the king alone, not George III only but his predecessors, too, each of whom had used his prerogative powers to extend the empire's military and commercial protection to the colonists in exchange for their pledge of obedience to him as the head of the empire.

Even though a lot of ink had been spilled by the Americans protesting against "taxation without representation," Parliament's asserted right to tax the colonists had nothing, or at least very little, to do with the casus belli, which was overwhelmingly the king's fault, according to the Declaration. Jefferson had been arguing this way for at least two years, since his 1774 pamphlet *A Summary View of the Rights of British America*. James Wilson had come to the same conclusion even earlier, in *Considerations on the Nature and Extent of the Legislative Authority of the British Parliament*, as had Franklin more discreetly; and the First Continental Congress, too, though with great reluctance. Hence the Declaration of Independence accuses the king of combining "with others to subject us to a jurisdiction foreign to our constitution, and unacknowledged by our laws; giving his Assent to their Acts of pretended legislation." The "others" referred to here means Parliament, an institution the Declaration refuses in its final form to dignify by even mentioning.[13] In its rough draft, however, the Committee had treated of Parliament's authority succinctly: "That in constituting indeed our several forms of government, we [the colonies] had adopted one common king... but that submission to their parliament was no part of our constitution."[14]

Natural Right and Political Right

But what then was "our constitution" to which the Declaration referred? No written constitution for America existed yet, nor would one be agreed to until the Articles of Confederation. (The committee to draw up the Articles of Confederation—one member from each state—had been appointed at the same time as the Committee of Five to draw up a declaration of independence, but the two did not cross paths; the Articles would not be drafted until 1777, nor ratified unanimously by the state legislatures until 1781.) After the Articles of Confederation would come, in due course, the Constitution of the United States, proposed in convention in Philadelphia in 1787 and adopted in 1788.

In the Declaration of Independence, "our constitution," with a lowercase "c," means the British constitution in America or the joint Anglo-American constitutional order as understood and, more or less, practiced in America. This was the unwritten or mostly unwritten constitution that incorporated the legal habits or norms of the British Empire, until those norms had been violated or contradicted, alas, by the empire's "pretended Legislation," since the Stamp Act. "Our constitution" included not only the positive laws or statutes passed by Parliament and the king, but also the Magna Carta and those rights of Englishmen secured by courts and juries, as well as the divisions of power between the mother country and the colonial governments, which were fundamental to the health and freedom of the empire. "Our constitution" thus extended also to the common law and those principles of natural justice or natural right (such as no taxation without representation) that informed or were supposed to inform the structure of the British form of government.

In its appeal to both positive (or legal) right and natural right, then, to "our constitution" and "our laws," the Declaration deploys a kind of Aristotelian argument. In one of his more enigmatic passages, Aristotle, in Book V of the *Nicomachean Ethics*, defines political right as partly natural and partly conventional or legal, suggesting that in politics natural right and conventional right come wrapped up together in concrete political situations.[15] The Declaration seems to agree with that suggestion, as least insofar as it moves from an account of pre-political natural rights to a defense of "the Right of the People" to choose a new form of government in or through politics, which form not only secures their individual natural rights but also embodies and enacts their *opinion* of what conduces to "their Safety and Happiness"—the alpha and omega of political life, as Aristotle and his tradition had argued. That is to say, those kind of judgments concerning what is required by the common good and the circumstances of political action are seen in the Declaration as complements or completions of natural right, in the sense that Aristotle might recognize as political right.

In the three days it spent editing the Committee of Five's version of the text, for example, the Congress tightened some and relaxed others of Jefferson's strictures against the king: George III's actions put the Americans under "the necessity which constrains them" not "to expunge" their former systems of government, as Jefferson had emphasized, but merely "to alter" them. Whereas Jefferson accused the king of "unremitting" injuries, the Congress preferred "repeated" injuries and dropped the charge that his conduct contained "no solitary fact to contradict the uniform tenor of the rest."[16] In one case, however, the Congress intensified Jefferson's charges. He had condemned the king's "transporting large Armies of foreign Mercenaries" to America. That was an act, Congress added, "scarcely paralleled in the most barbarous ages" and "totally"—Congress's term—"unworthy the Head of a civilized nation." Thus Congress emphasized Jefferson's own recognition that barbarism was possible even in very advanced or civilized nations and times and went beyond his recognition by specifying that modern barbarism could be even worse than primitive barbarism.

Above all, the Committee of the Whole balked at Jefferson's long discussion of the slave trade. In notes made at the time, Jefferson blamed the decision on "complaisance" to South Carolina and Georgia, which needed more slaves and wanted the slave trade to flourish, and on the consent of "Northern brethren" who did not own many slaves but had been "pretty considerable carriers of them to others."[17] There seemed to be sufficient guilt to go around, in short, without coming to Jefferson's conclusion that the king alone or in particular deserved to be condemned for allowing the slave trade to continue. But that is the tack he took. "He has waged cruel war against human nature itself," Jefferson declared,

> violating its most sacred rights of life and liberty in the persons of a distant people, who never offended him, captivating and carrying them into slavery in another hemisphere.... This piratical warfare, the opprobrium of *infidel* powers, is the warfare of the *Christian* king of Great Britain, determined to keep open a market where MEN should be bought & sold, he has prostituted his negative [i.e., his royal veto] for suppressing every legislative attempt to prohibit or to restrain this execrable commerce.[18] (Emphasis in original.)

Admittedly, it would be useful in our contemporary debates over the 1619 Project and similar attempts to simplify our thinking about slavery and the founders if we could point to words in the Declaration that explicitly identify blacks as MEN (all capitals)—that is, human beings—too (and which also implicitly identify black women as human beings), as well as words that condemn slavery as unjust because it is an unholy violation of humanity's rights to life and liberty.

Jefferson's proposed words, which did all that, would also have fed an interesting debate about Islam's responsibility for promoting slavery and the slave trade; the "infidel powers" referred to are, of course, mainly Muslims. But that George III deserved to be blamed for fostering the slave trade because he was a bad "Christian king" who wouldn't approve Virginia's and a few other colonies' efforts to outlaw or regulate the slave trade is a stretch. For one thing, it leaves out those states, such as South Carolina and Georgia, that persistently favored a more robust market "where MEN should be bought and sold."

Jefferson was not finished, however. "And that this assemblage of horrors might want no fact of distinguished die," he continued in the deleted paragraph,

> he [George III] now is exciting those very people, to rise in arms among us, and to purchase that liberty of which *he* has deprived them, by murdering the people among whom *he* has also obtruded them: thus paying off former crimes committed against the *liberties* of one people, with crimes which he urges them to commit against the *lives* of another.[19] (Emphasis in original.)

Here was an echo of the offer by Lord Dunmore, the royal governor of Virginia, to free any slaves who were willing to join the British army's war against the Patriots. (The Congress also included an earlier indictment against George III for exciting "domestic insurrection amongst us," meaning among our fellow citizens, not just slaves.)[20]

Despite the advantages that Jefferson's language would have brought to future discussions, the Congress did not hesitate to strike out the entire paragraph. It was, we may conjecture, over the top; too good to be true; too clever by half. Jefferson was effectively claiming in this paragraph, after all, that neither America as a whole nor, say, Virginia in particular was responsible, even partly, for the slave trade and slavery. That those were at worst South Carolina and Georgia's fault. Before all, they were the king's fault. George III saw to it that blacks were brought from Africa in chains, and then he offered to have those chains removed only if the blacks would kill their former masters. Whether offering enslavement or emancipation, the king was in the wrong. The Americans were more or less innocent victims of his tyrannical ploys. Jefferson's interpretation of events came close to what today we would call virtue signaling. Whichever way the king turned, he was on the wrong side of history, and the Americans were on the right side.

Jefferson meant for this last item in his long indictment of George III to be its climax. He saved the most awful words to describe it— "murdering," "piratical warfare," "opprobrium," and "execrable commerce," and he still had to resort to italics and capital letters to convey his horror. His indignation at having it eighty-sixed by the Congress was deep-rooted. Jefferson's heartfelt crescendo had something to do with his desire, shared in a slightly different way with Paine, to draw a bright line between Britain's mixed regime and America's new republican ones, between hereditary and elective political authority, between Britain's past and America's future, between the Old World and the New. Adams has his own way to describe that difference, as we shall see.

For its part, the Committee of the Whole apparently did not believe that the question of slavery was ripe for such a summary discussion, nor that a philippic against it, to borrow Adams's term, would help persuade other countries to support the American war for independence, which after all was a principal aim of the Declaration. With the self-evident truth that all men are created equal already declared, there was little or no doubt about the wrongness of slavery in the abstract—that is, as a question of natural right. The question concerned what to do about slavery as a matter of political right.

A Memorable Epoch

The Congress was not through with its editorial work. It tinkered with the draft's penultimate paragraph and then boldly rewrote the final paragraph. The former concerned the American revolutionaries' relation to the British people they were leaving behind, as opposed to the guilty king whom they had spent many paragraphs, the whole central section, denouncing. The Committee of Five concluded the next-to-last paragraph with a kind of valedictory:

> We might have been a free & a great people together; but a communication of grandeur & of freedom it seems is below their dignity. Be it so, since they will have it: the road to happiness & to glory is open to us too; we will climb it apart from them, and acquiesce in the necessity which denounces our eternal separation![21]

The Congress struck almost all these sentiments, including the exclamation point—the draft's only one. Perhaps having excised the long paragraph on slavery and the slave trade, the Congress felt keenly the hypocrisy or awkwardness of now celebrating, even by comparison with the British people, the Americans' grandeur, freedom, happiness, and glory. The Committee of the Whole retained only the sober parting words,

> We have appealed to their native justice and magnanimity, and we have conjured them by the ties of our common kindred.... They too have been deaf to the voice of justice and of consanguinity. We must, therefore, acquiesce in the necessity, which denounces our Separation, and hold them, as we hold the rest of mankind, Enemies in War, in Peace Friends.

The final paragraph's tone is higher, more honorable. Jefferson had always intended for the Declaration to end with the phrase "sacred honor," and indeed from the first he had it closing with the triad, "And for the support of this Declaration, we mutually pledge to each other our Lives, our Fortunes, & our sacred Honor."[22] The Congress interposed two changes, two invocations of God. To the first sentence of the closing paragraph it added, after this noun of address, "We, therefore, the Representatives of the United states of america, in General Congress, Assembled," the phrase "appealing to the Supreme Judge of the world for the rectitude of our intentions." To the final sentence of the paragraph, the Congress added, after the words "and for the support of this Declaration," the phrase "with a firm reliance on the protection of divine Providence."

The Declaration in its final form contains five references to God, broadly speaking. Three came from the Committee of Five, two in the opening two paragraphs of its draft—"the Laws of Nature and of Nature's God" in the first paragraph and "all men are created equal" and "endowed by their Creator with certain unalienable Rights" in the second—and one from the draft's closing sentence ("sacred Honor"). The other two references to God came from the Congress—namely, "appealing to the Supreme Judge of the world" and "with a firm reliance on the protection of divine Providence." The Committee of the Whole's edits thus produced a marked increase in the religiosity of the Declaration. If we count only more or less explicit invocations of the living God, calling Him by one of His names (legislator, Creator, Supreme Judge, and divine Providence), the Congress inserted fully half, two of the four. (Strictly speaking, "sacred Honor," though compatible with the biblical God, does not imply or require Him.)[23] In any case, the Declaration is difficult to defend as a purely deistic document, especially after the Congress's editorial changes to it.

Less often remarked is how what one might call the moral tone of the Declaration revealed itself in the course of its editing. The Declaration pays "a decent respect to the opinions of mankind"—not to mankind's passions or interests, so that, by the famous definition of *Federalist* 10, for example, the Declaration cannot be accused of stirring up a popular faction against the British government or against government in general. There is a public-spiritedness or a high-mindedness to the Declaration. It stakes its case on "certain unalienable rights" and "self-evident" truths; it declines to derive those rights from the desire for self-preservation or from any anterior passions, much less from the prevailing culture or values. In the Declaration, human equality tends to be seen in the light of the high rather than the low—in the light of opinions, of humans' "endowment" with rights and reason, of God as Creator, Judge, Legislator, and Providence, and of the duty to risk life and fortune for sacred honor. That closing vow in the Declaration's concluding sentence is made by its signers to "each other," not to the people or to mankind or to the right side of history.

During its editing, the Declaration's appeals to the sacred, to what is high in the sense of holy or godly, shifted noticeably. At first, the Committee of Five hailed "these truths," including human equality, as "sacred and undeniable."[24] They thought better of that and tightened the holy of holies to a subset of *self-evident* truths. In the term's next appearance, Jefferson condemned the king for waging "cruel war against human nature itself, violating its most sacred rights of life & liberty in the persons of a distant people who never offended him, captivating and carrying them into slavery."[25] The distinction between the "most sacred" and less sacred human rights may have proved inconvenient or slippery.

After the Congress had removed the whole discussion of slavery, only a single mention of "sacred" remained in the Declaration: "And for the support of this Declaration, with a firm reliance on the protection of divine Providence, we mutually pledge to each other our Lives, our Fortunes and our sacred Honor." Here, the document implies that our lives and fortunes are *less* sacred or valuable than our honor. Admittedly, "honor" is closer to "liberty" as a concept than to life and fortune, combining the disdain of the honor lover for mere life or mere prosperity with the risk-taking traits of the freedom lover. In any case, the Declaration's signers distinguish themselves as a group or elite, inter alia, by taking *responsibility* for holding "these truths to be self-evident," for asserting human equality and capacity for self-government, and in particular by assembling the case that George III is pursuing a "design to reduce them under absolute Despotism," and hence that it is now "their right, it is their duty" to overthrow his government and institute a new one. That coincidence of right and duty speaks not only to the honor of the signers or founders but also to their virtue. As Adams explained in *Thoughts on Government*, "Honor is truly sacred, but holds a lower rank in the scale of moral excellence than virtue."[26]

Jefferson's reliance on Franklin and Adams among the Committee of Five was not merely because of his friends' genius but also, to be sure, because their votes gave him three out of five—a majority of the committee. No interpretation of the Declaration's writing and editing could ignore that elementary fact. Likewise, no interpretation of the Declaration could ignore the well-known facts that the remarkable consensus of opinion embodied in the Declaration of Independence, and likewise the later remarkable unanimity hailed in *The Federalist* as informing the writing and ratification of the US Constitution, were succeeded rapidly by the bitter partisan battles of the 1790s. Or how, in turn, that decade of partisan warfare was itself quickly succeeded by the collapse of Adams's Federalist Party and, in fact, the virtual disappearance of party conflict in general temporarily in the so-called Era of Good Feelings. At least one distant root of these later partisan disagreements and reunifications is already visible in the way Adams and Jefferson talked about their magnificent joint handiwork—the Declaration.

Admittedly, it is easy to read the later disagreements back into 1776—and I would not go so far as, say, Danielle Allen does in distinguishing what she calls the Adams Declaration (which is, at any rate, not our Declaration of Independence but rather a proclamation from the Massachusetts General Court, drafted by Adams in January 19, 1776) from Jefferson's Declaration.[27] Still, as they approached the 50th anniversary of the great document and as they contemplated the prospect of their own death, the two main authors and editors of the Declaration sized up its significance very differently.

Jefferson's letter to Roger Weightman (on June 24, 1826) as he was declining due to ill health the invitation to visit Washington, DC, on July 4, 1826, is well-known. He saluted the Declaration with his characteristic faith or hope in human progress. "May it be to the world," he wrote,

> what I believe it will be, (to some parts sooner, to others later, but finally to all.) the Signal of arousing men to burst the chains, under which Monkish ignorance and superstition had persuaded them to bind themselves, and to assume the blessings and security of self government.... All eyes are opened, or opening to the rights of man. the general spread of the light of science has already laid open to every view the palpable truth that the mass of mankind has not been born, with saddles on their backs, nor a favored few booted and spurred, ready to ride them legitimately, by the grace of god.[28]

Much less well-known is Adams's reply to John Whitney, on June 7, 1826. Whitney, the mayor of Quincy, Massachusetts, where Adams lived, had invited Adams to a similar celebration of the anniversary there. Adams declined to attend, for the same reason as Jefferson, but left the following written tribute. The 50 years since independence he hailed as "a Memorable epoch in the annals of the human race; destined, in future history, to form the brightest or the blackest page, according to the use or the abuse of those political institutions by which they shall, in time to come, be Shaped, by the *human mind.*"[29] (Emphasis in original.)

No promise of worldwide liberation or enlightenment, no suggestion that palpable or scientific truths would come to the rescue of self-evident or moral truths, no claim that the human mind would prove permanently or inevitably progressive, but instead a sober prediction that the future will be like the past in terms of reason's susceptibility to virtue and vice and, hence, humanity's susceptibility to both good government and misgovernment.

This is not to suggest that Jefferson and Adams offered competing or incompatible visions of what the Declaration had to say. Both men, in fact, shared a core understanding of natural right as the human being's or the rational animal's (at least *rationis capax*, as Jonathan Swift reminded that generation) participation in morality; but their own political opinions and judgments added or subtracted from that core to yield discrepant versions of political right. Jefferson understood, as Adams did, that no human being had by nature the right to rule another as any human had the right to rule a horse or other brute creature—that was the enduring core of natural right and rights. But Jefferson understood this to be a kind of Enlightenment discovery, a token of "the general spread of the light of science."

When Adams was asked about this by his son, Charles, in 1794, he replied that the "modern doctrine of equality" is in truth based on "that eternal and fundamental Principle of the Law of Nature, Do as you would be done by and Love your Neighbor as yourself." The modern doctrine of equality was thus as old as Christianity, if not older. "How the present Age can boast of this Principle as a Discovery, as new Light and modern Knowledge I know not." By equality Adams meant "not a physical but a moral equality . . . all equally in the Same Cases intitled to the Same Justice."[30]

For Jefferson, natural right, though based in natural species and their permanent differences, was to some extent forward-looking, a projection of the movement from the state of nature into civil society and onward to tomorrow's civil society. For Adams, the permanence of nature, and particularly of human nature, with its cognate customs and institutions, was more profound. Neither founder thought that, for example, the distinction between a horse and a human being was transitory or a mere 18th-century relation. But that left them plenty to argue over.

Both sought to build the American republic on long-standing American foundations—whether laid by the Pilgrims or by virtuous yeoman farmers. Neither was prepared to rely merely on a state of nature filled with abstract, unconnected masterless men. Their statesmanship sought to ground citizens in a concrete American civic project. And the Declaration of Independence, as authored and edited by them above all, declared that project to the world.

Notes

1. Thomas Jefferson to Henry Lee, May 8, 1825, Founders Online, https://founders.archives.gov/documents/Jefferson/98-01-02-5212.

2. See Pauline Maier, *American Scripture: Making the Declaration of Independence* (Vintage Books, 1998), 99–104. See also *The Papers of Thomas Jefferson*, ed. Julian P. Boyd, vol. 1, *1760–1776* (Princeton University Press, 1950), 413–33. For photographic reproductions of the known drafts of the document, compare Julian P. Boyd, *The Declaration of Independence: The Evolution of the Text*, rev. ed., ed. Gerald W. Gawalt (Library of Congress, 1999).

3. Becker observes in a footnote to the insertion of "self-evident" into the Committee of Five's draft that "it is not clear that this change was made by Jefferson. The handwriting of 'self-evident' resembles Franklin's." He never mentions this uncertainty again. Indeed, much later in his book he writes confidently, "When Jefferson submitted the draft to Adams the only correction he had made was to write 'self-evident' in place of 'sacred & undeniable.'" Carl L. Becker, *The Declaration of Independence: A Study in the History of Political Ideas* (1922; Vintage Books, 1970), 142, 198; and Maier, *American Scripture*, 136.

4. See Robert Ginsberg, "The Declaration as Rhetoric," in *A Casebook on the Declaration of Independence: Analysis of the Structure, Meaning, and Literary Worth of the Text*, ed. Robert Ginsberg (Thomas Y. Crowell, 1967), 234–35.

5. For Jefferson's original draft of the Declaration, see *The Papers of Thomas Jefferson*, 1:243–47.

6. Becker, *The Declaration of Independence*, 198.

7. Maier, *American Scripture*, 151.

8. See Maier, *American Scripture*, 149; and Becker, *The Declaration of Independence*, 208–9.

9. Maier, *American Scripture*, 122–23.

10. John Adams, *The Adams Papers*, ed. L. H. Butterfield (Harvard University Press, 1961), 3:357–59.

11. Thomas Paine, *Common Sense*, in *Paine: Political Writings*, ed. Bruce Kuklick (Cambridge University Press, 2000), 5.

12. Adams, *The Adams Papers*, 385–86.

13. Perhaps the most lucid interpretation of the Americans' development of "the theory of the British empire" remains that in Becker, *The Declaration of Independence*, ch. 3.

14. See Becker, *The Declaration of Independence*, 168.

15. Aristotle, *Nicomachean Ethics*, trans. Robert C. Bartlett and Susan D. Collins (University of Chicago Press, 2011), 1134b18–19. "Of the just in the political sense, one part is natural, the other, conventional."

16. *The Papers of Thomas Jefferson*, 1:245.

17. See Becker, *The Declaration of Independence*, 212–23.

18. *The Papers of Thomas Jefferson*, 1:246–47.
19. *The Papers of Thomas Jefferson*, 1:247.
20. Maier, *American Scripture*, 147.
21. *The Papers of Thomas Jefferson*, 1:426.
22. *The Papers of Thomas Jefferson*, 1:247.
23. Compare Danielle Allen, *Our Declaration: A Reading of the Declaration of Independence in Defense of Equality* (Liveright, 2014), 115–18.
24. *The Papers of Thomas Jefferson*, 1:426.
25. *The Papers of Thomas Jefferson*, 1:247.
26. See Danielle Allen, "The Adams Declaration: A Guide for Our Times," in *Democracy and the American Revolution*, ed. Yuval Levin et al. (AEI Press, 2024).
27. John Adams, "Thoughts on Government," in *The Political Writings of John Adams*, ed. George W. Carey (Regnery, 2000), 483.
28. Thomas Jefferson to Roger Chew Weightman, June 24, 1826, Founders Online, https://founders.archives.gov/documents/Jefferson/98-01-02-6179.
29. John Adams to John Whitney, June 7, 1826, Founders Online, https://founders.archives.gov/documents/Adams/99-02-02-8023.
30. John Adams to Charles Adams, January 9, 1794, in *John Adams: Writings from the New Nation, 1784–1826*, ed. Gordon S. Wood (Library of America, 2016), 300–1.

3

Equality, Liberty, and Rights in the Declaration of Independence

MICHAEL ZUCKERT

Strictly speaking, the document we call the Declaration of Independence is misnamed. The actual or official declaration of independence occurred on July 2, 1776, when the Second Continental Congress adopted the resolution for independence introduced a month earlier by Virginian Richard Henry Lee. The relevant part of Lee's resolution was incorporated in the July 4 document near its end:

> That these United Colonies are, and of Right ought to be Free and Independent States; that they are Absolved from all Allegiance to the British Crown, and that all political connection between them and the State of Great Britain, is and ought to be totally dissolved.

What then is the so-called Declaration of Independence? The opening sentence of that document announces its aim: Acting with "a decent respect to the opinions of mankind," the Americans propose to "declare the causes which impel them to the separation." A better title for our document, then, would be "The Declaration of the Causes Which Impel the Americans to Declare Independence."

The Structure of the Declaration

As a declaration of causes meant to explain and justify the Americans in the eyes of the world in terms of "The Laws of Nature and of Nature's

God," the Declaration of Independence (let us stick to its traditional title) intended to show the "causes" in the sense of the impelling reasons for the Americans' actions and the "causes" in the sense of moral justification for their action. The Declaration thus contains not only much historical information relating to the recent relations between Britain and the colonies but also a general theory of political right meant to show the colonists to be justified even in the eyes of "the Supreme Judge of the world."

This justificatory intention dictates the general structure of the Declaration. It takes the form of a long but recognizable syllogism. After an opening paragraph announcing the authors' intention in the document, the Declaration proceeds to lay out the major premises of its argument, presented here as "truths" held to be "self-evident" by the colonists, the final one of which proclaims that "whenever any Form of Government becomes destructive of these ends [for which government is instituted], it is the Right of the People to alter or to abolish it, and to institute new Government."

Following this major premise is a series of "Facts . . . submitted to a candid world," purporting to show that the government under which the British held the colonies was one that was indeed "destructive of these ends." If that is so, then the conclusion, introduced by the word "therefore," "that these United Colonies are, and of Right ought to be Free and Independent States," follows with the logical necessity of a geometric proof. Contrary to the opinion of some scholars that the parts of the Declaration are disparate and of unequal importance, the main parts—the theory of rightful government contained in the major premises of the second paragraph and the list of grievances comprising the minor premise—are integrally connected and equally essential to accomplishing the aim of the document.[1]

I begin with the syllogistic character of the Declaration, for too often this is missed and the various ideas present in it, especially in its second or theoretical paragraph, are taken as separate nuggets and interpreted in a free-floating way, independently of the rest. This is particularly true of such resonant ideas as the first of the so-called self-evident truths: "All men are created equal." Throughout American history, this phrase has been treated as especially important, and many of the hopes and aspirations of various political movements have been projected onto these five words. Most notable, probably, has been Abraham Lincoln's quotation of them in his best-known speech: "Four score and seven years ago our fathers brought forth on this continent a new nation, conceived in liberty, and dedicated to the proposition that all men are created equal." This was a prelude to his call for a "new birth of freedom,"[2] to be effected through the liberation of the enslaved persons he had begun to achieve in his Emancipation Proclamation.

But the equality clause has been appealed to on many more occasions, often with quite different applications. Sometimes, as with Lincoln, it is taken as a call for natural equality—that is, for recognition of a universal human status that rules slavery out of court. Sometimes, as with the early women's movement, it is seen as a call for full civil equality—for recognition of a civil status contrary to the disabilities from which women suffered. Sometimes it is taken to be a call for economic equality or equality of condition, such as is held to be inconsistent with great social and economic inequalities. Ripped from its context as part of the major premise of a great syllogism, the equality proposition is rendered quite indeterminate in meaning and becomes subject to this great variety of interpretive and political appropriations. One recent study even found "five facets" of equality in the Declaration, a lot of work for one small word.[3]

As part of the major premise of the Declaration's syllogism and a general theory of rightful government, it is unlikely that the main ideas in the Declaration's second paragraph exist as separate, free-floating nuggets of indeterminate meaning. My task in this chapter is to reconstruct the theory of rightful government contained in that paragraph to progress toward fixing meaning for those ideas—equality, rights, liberty, and others—that have been so important to the self-understanding and political aspirations of Americans from 1776 on.

Contributing in no small degree to the notion that the big ideas in the second paragraph are separate nuggets is the way the text introduces them: "We hold these truths to be self-evident," a clause then followed by a list of six identifiable truths that, so introduced, might appear to be just six independent, separate truths. But if we set aside the claim about self-evidence for a moment, we can readily see that the six truths are not separate and disconnected. We can paraphrase the six in the following shorthand manner:

1. All men are created equal.

2. They are endowed with unalienable rights, among which are life, liberty, and pursuit of happiness.

3. Governments are instituted among men to secure these rights.

4. Governments derive their just powers from the consent of the governed.

5. If governments fail at their instituted purpose of securing these rights, the people have a right to alter or abolish them—that is, a right of revolution.

6. The people then have a right to institute new governments, which in their judgment will succeed better in providing the security of rights for which they made government in the first place.

The list appears to have a distinctly temporal character. It begins by announcing how things are at the beginning, at creation: At the beginning human beings are equal, and they possess certain rights. The next two truths tell of the sequel—human beings institute government to "secure" these rights with which they are born. Government is necessary because in the conditions at the beginning, the rights are insecure. So, the second set of truths tells us why governments exist and how they rightfully come to have their powers: via "consent of the governed."

The governed are particularly central to the enterprise of government, for it is the securing of their rights that serves as the purpose of governmental institution, and their consent is the means by which rightful government comes to be. So, we can draw a conclusion about the relations among the first four truths: The second two tell of the formation of government as a remedy to a deficiency of the pre-governmental situation. The first two truths, therefore, must refer to a situation in which there is no government, and thus in which rights are insecure.

The last two truths speak of a situation subsequent to the institution of government. The mere existence of government does not guarantee the security of rights for the sake of which government is desired. Government can fail at its appointed task. When it does, the people have the right to change or even throw off their government. Since they would then find themselves with no government, and therefore once again with the insecurity of rights, they have the same right to make new governments that they had at the beginning, which we can now see need not mean some absolute beginning but the beginning of a cycle of no government, then government instituting, then government altering or abolishing, and back to the beginning.

This last set of truths is particularly important, as Pauline Maier has pointed out, for it is the altering or (in this case) "abolishing" that the Americans are attempting to explain and justify in their Declaration.[4] Given the temporally sequential character of the list of rights, it is obvious that the fifth truth affirming a right to "alter or abolish" is connected to, and could even be said to follow from, the truths that precede it. Indeed, we can look at the list of truths as an argument in which each set of two truths follows logically (not just temporally) from the truths ahead of them on the list.

Equality, Rights, and Property

To understand the logic of the second paragraph, we must put aside for the moment the temporality of the sequence of truth claims we have so far been using to make sense of the text. The first two truths clearly speak of something original: how men were at the beginning ("created equal") and what they possessed at the beginning ("endowed by their Creator with certain unalienable Rights"). On reflection, these claims cannot refer to a strictly temporal beginning or origin, for they are said to refer to "all men"—that is to say, not just to those who stand at the very beginning, literally before government was instituted. All men, whether born into a society already possessing government or somehow not, are "created equal" and possess rights not deriving from or dependent for their existence on government.

The claim that governments are instituted via consent of the governed gives a clue as to how to understand these puzzling claims: Governments derive their "just powers," their rightful power to command and expect obedience, not from any inherent right they possess but only from the consent of the citizens subject to that government. If that is so, one can translate the claim that all men are created equal into the claim that no man is born naturally or originally subject to government or owing obedience to government. We are all originally equal in that nobody possesses inherent authority over us.

This is the same claim that political philosophers of the age stated with the idea of an original "state of nature." John Locke defined that state as one "*of Equality*, wherein all the Power and Jurisdiction is reciprocal, no one having more than another."[5] (Emphasis in original.) The equality in question is equality in "power and jurisdiction"—that is, in authority or the right to command others. In authority all are by nature equal, and they are equal in having no authority over others, for it is "a *State of perfect Freedom* to order their Actions . . . as they think fit, . . . without asking leave, or depending upon the Will of any other Man."[6] (Emphasis in original.)

Placing the first truth about equality in the context of the political theory outlined in the Declaration's second paragraph leads us to see that equality there has a quite precise and even radical meaning: Human beings are not *naturally* subject to the authority of any other human being. Whatever the ultimate implications of this natural equality may be, we can see that the Declaration is not invoking a loose concept ready to be filled in as we please, as it has sometimes been treated.

Nonetheless, the affirmation of natural equality immediately raises two urgent questions. First, on what basis is this equality affirmed? It is clearly not the result of immediate empirical observation, because most are born under government and thought to be subject to the authority of that government, an observation that has led many political thinkers, such as Aristotle in particular, to pronounce political authority natural. The second urgent question arises from the observation that this natural equality, this situation of non-subjection to any human authority, does not persist, for the text of the second paragraph quickly moves on to affirm the existence of "rightful powers" of government. But just how does the original non-subjection transform into subjection?

In attempting to answer these two questions, we must remind ourselves of the kind of text the Declaration is—and isn't. The purpose of the text, you may recall, is to "declare the causes" for the Americans' separation from the authority to whom they have heretofore owed obedience. It is a giving of reasons, not a mere assertion of will. That is why it takes the form of an argument. But it is still a political document; it is not a treatise in political philosophy. The Declaration presents an argument to justify the deeds of the Americans, but it is a truncated presentation of an argument that perhaps would require a treatise to make its case fully. We must tailor our expectations of the Declaration accordingly. Among other things, that means one has to do some real work to expand the concisely expressed elements of the Declaration's argument.

In the pre-governmental situation, human beings are equal, and they also possess rights. One common way to put together these two ideas is to claim, as Lincoln did, that the Declaration is affirming equality of a certain sort—equality in rights.[7] No doubt, since all human beings have the same rights, this is correct, but it misses the particular sense of equality affirmed. There is another and more promising way to connect these two aspects of the original situation, which at the same time provides an answer to our question about the grounds for the affirmation of human equality.

The Declaration lists three rights as among the inherent or natural rights human beings possess in a state of nature: rights to life, liberty, and pursuit of happiness. There are clearly others, such as the "right to alter or abolish" governments, affirmed a bit later in the paragraph; the right to liberty of conscience, as frequently affirmed by members of the founding generation; and the right to property, universally affirmed. Why are these three rights singled out for mention? It is difficult to give a definitive answer to that question, but it is plausible to say that these, along with the right "to alter or to abolish," were the most relevant to the task of justifying American independence.

In any case, we can see a kind of coherence and deep complementarity to the list of rights presented. The right to life is a right to what is most one's own—one's life. Given the nature of a human life, it is difficult to see how it could be anything other than one's own, how it could in any sense belong to others. Given the dependence (or base) of life in or on the body, the right to life must contain a right to bodily immunity, the right not to have one's body seized, invaded, assaulted, or controlled by others.

The right to liberty extends the right to life: Not only does one possess a rightful immunity against depredations by others on one's body, but one also has a right to the use of one's body. We can take control of our bodies, or of parts of our bodies, to produce voluntary motion. We can invest our bodies' movements with our intentions and broader purposes. The natural right to liberty affirms the prima facie rightfulness of active, intentional use of the body. This is to say that the right to liberty contains more than the narrow right not to be imprisoned, through it surely includes that. There is something more positive as well to the right to liberty—the right to exercise our faculties as we see fit—always with the caveat that the same right in others must be respected.

The text does not directly affirm the right to property, often conjoined to the rights to life and liberty in common lists of rights. Its absence from this list has led to speculation that the authors of the Declaration did not mean to affirm a natural right to property. This seems doubtful in light of all the documents of the age, including many by Thomas Jefferson, the chief draftsman of the Declaration, that affirm the natural right to property.[8]

Moreover, the natural right to property is implicit elsewhere in the Declaration's text, when the Americans complain of the British attempt to tax them without their consent. This concern, well-known to be one of the most significant colonial grievances, as captured in the slogan "No taxation without representation," implies the recognition of a natural right to property, for it is that status that led the Americans to conclude that they must themselves be represented in the body that taxes them. That is to say, the Americans interpreted the no-taxation-without-representation requirement of the traditional English constitution differently from the way the English themselves did because they clearly and unequivocally saw property to be a natural right.[9] The tacitly present right to property involves an extension of rights from the spheres of one's own life, body, and actions to the external world. It proclaims the rightful power of human beings to make the external their own in the same way that they can make their bodies their own.

The three basic rights together thus amount to the affirmation of a kind of personal sovereignty—rightful control over one's person, actions, and possessions in the service of one's intents and purposes. When seen as an integrated system of immunities and controls, the specific rights sum to a comprehensive right to pursue a self-chosen shape and way of life. The comprehensive or summative character of the right to pursuit of happiness extends and subsumes the other rights.

The comprehensive character of the system of rights, as summed up in the right to pursuit of happiness, implies a kind of individual sovereignty and therewith a way to understand the ground for the affirmation of natural equality. If there is by nature a personal right to pursuit of happiness—that is, a right to pursue a shape of life for oneself, and one self-chosen (within the boundaries of the parallel rights of others and the needs of society)—then human beings must be equal in the sense affirmed. The personal right to pursue happiness is incompatible in its nature with natural subjection to another. Natural equality is thus a correlate of or even a derivation from the natural rights specified in the Declaration.

The two first truths are thus tightly and logically linked. If we push our inquiry about grounds for equality to rights, we reach a dead end. The Declaration itself does not tell us how we know that human beings bear rights or just what rights to include in the list of natural rights. Perhaps we can learn more when we examine the overarching claim that these truths are, or rather, are held to be "self-evident."

Equality of Whom?

Before we move on to our second question of how the theory of the Declaration gets from a state of no authority to an institution that has "just powers" and thus abrogates the original equality, we must pause to interrogate the equality claim at greater length. A frequently raised objection to the Declaration in the 20th and 21st centuries is that the Declaration may say equality of all, but it does not really mean it—that it means, for example, equality of white men only, excluding persons of other races and genders.

The assertion that the Declaration's proclamation of equality excludes persons of other races was forcefully raised in the years leading up to the Civil War as a response to abolitionist appeals to the "created equal" phrase in their attacks on slavery. The most notorious denial of the inclusion of the slaves and all blacks from the equality claim in the Declaration came in the *Dred Scott v. Sandford* case in the Supreme Court opinion by Chief Justice Roger B. Taney, who concluded that neither the language of the Declaration nor the protections in the Constitution applied to the black race: Blacks, he said, "had no rights which the white man was bound to respect."[10]

Taney attributed this view to the authors of the Declaration: How could they affirm the natural rights of blacks and at the same time hold so many in slavery? Jefferson, a slaveholder to be sure, did not agree with Taney. In his draft of the Declaration, he condemned the king for having "waged cruel war against human nature itself, violating its most sacred rights of life and liberty in the persons of a distant people who never offended him, captivating them and carrying them into slavery in another hemisphere." Jefferson added that the king was "determined to keep open a market where MEN should be bought and sold."[11] (Emphasis in original.) There is thus no doubt that Jefferson considered the blacks to be men and therefore included in the meaning of the Declaration's language. So, Jefferson the slaveholder could write of American slavery in his *Notes on the State of Virginia*, "I tremble for my country when I reflect that God is just: that his justice cannot sleep forever." He feared a coming race war, of which he observes that "the Almighty has no attribute which can take side with us in such a contest."[12]

Some years later, he spoke again of slavery in these terms:

> The love of justice and the love of country plead equally the cause of these people, and it is a moral reproach to us that they should have pleaded it so long in vain, and should have produced not a single effort . . . to relieve them & ourselves from our present condition of moral & political reprobation.[13]

Jefferson and other American declarers of independence may have been slaveholders, but they were guilty reprobates in their own eyes. How best to understand the simultaneous condemnation and continuance of slavery is a worthy question, the answering of which goes beyond the scope of this chapter, but there can be little doubt that the Americans, then and now, have understood blacks to be included in the "all men" who are "created equal."

And women? Are they included in "all men?" It is sometimes doubted that women were included, in part because of that ambiguous term "men," but even more because of the various civil and political disabilities under which women suffered in 1776. Could the authors of the Declaration mean to pronounce women equal when they were denied the rights to vote, serve on juries, hold political office, and pursue certain professions? Without denying the importance of these civil and political disabilities, it is necessary to note the bearing of the Declaration's affirmation of universal human equality: It applies to a pre-political or perhaps nonpolitical situation. It is an attempt to consider the human endowment outside of, irrespective of, and ultimately constitutive for the political.

Note that none of the rights listed in this part of the Declaration are political rights, which makes perfect sense because these are rights held independently of the existence of government. They are natural as opposed to civil or political rights. Understood in this way, it is difficult to deny that women are included, for their basic natural rights were indeed recognized in 1776. The law, for example, recognizes women as possessing a right to life insofar as it forbids the taking of a woman's life as much as it does a man's. Now it remains an important question, unsettled in the Declaration itself or by the founding generation, what the original equality and possession of rights implies about civil and political rights. This is a question that has been and still is being worked out in the American political tradition.

Consent and Revolution

As we move to the second set of truths, those that sketch the why and how of the institution of government, we are forced to notice that there is a suppressed or underdeveloped premise in the argument. The text tells us: "To secure these rights, Governments are instituted among Men." This implies that without government these natural rights are insecure, but we are given no further information as to why that is so.

In the political-philosophical literature that the Declaration's theory so closely resembles, much space is devoted to discussing why the state of equality, the state of human life without government, would render rights insecure. The chief philosophers agree on the fact but disagree on the reasons for rights insecurity. The Declaration takes no sides on whether Locke or Thomas Hobbes, to take two important examples, is more correct on the reason for the unviability of the state of nature. The

Declaration, however, agrees with the philosophers in the chief point they extract from thinking about human life without government and thus of coming to understand why government is needed.

The point they all agree on can most perspicuously be restated as follows: Even though all human beings are endowed by nature or God with natural rights, these rights will tend not to be respected by others absent the existence in society of an institution armed with legitimate coercive authority, with which it can pass laws to protect and exercise the muscle to see that these laws are enforced. They agree, in a word, that the state of strict equality as a state of no rule is not a viable human condition; neither a situation in which no one can rightfully coerce others nor one in which all can rightfully coerce produces a situation in which the rights of all are respected. So a specialized institution to exercise coercion on behalf of rights—that is, government—is needed.

Thus, the tight logic of the Declaration continues into the second set of truths so long as we note the underdeveloped premise of rights insecurity in the condition of equality. The governments instituted among men derive "their just powers from the consent of the governed." The way in which this claim follows from the precedent truths is evident when we take seriously the implication of the original equality: That men are created equal means there is no natural basis for political authority; contrary to a long tradition that held otherwise, the Declaration is affirming that neither God nor nature has ordained or appointed government or governors. Since there is no natural or divine source of authority, the people forming the government must be the source of its rightful powers. Only they can remove themselves from their primitive condition of non-subjection to one of subjection to government.

This action by the governed is described as consent, but exactly how this consent is expressed is not stated. The reason for this silence is relatively easy to discern: The immediate goal of the document is to justify the act of rebellion that is the declaring of independence. This is an act not of giving but of withdrawing consent. In a sense the act of rightfully withdrawing consent is nothing other than refusing to recognize the existing authorities as legitimate and withholding obedience to their laws and other actions. Conversely, the act of consenting to government must involve at least recognizing government and governmental authorities and willingly obeying their laws and other actions.

It is often thought that the truth about consent implies the sole legitimacy of democracy as the rightful form of government. That conclusion is certainly understandable, but it is not well supported by the Declaration's text. As the last of the Declaration's six truths pronounces, the people in the postrevolutionary situation, having altered or abolished the existing government, have "the Right . . . to institute new Government, laying its foundation on such principles and organizing its powers in such form, as to them shall seem most likely to effect their Safety and Happiness." The theory of the Declaration does not commit to one form of government as solely legitimate but is quite open-ended in leaving it up to each people to decide for itself, in light of its own situation and traditions.

Indeed, the text even proclaims an openness to monarchy, the kind of government the Americans were in the process of throwing off. After listing the grievances against the king, the text concludes that "a Prince, whose character is thus marked by every act which may define a Tyrant, is unfit to be the ruler of a free people." It follows then that a prince who is not a tyrant, who respects and secures the rights for the sake of which government exists, could well be a fit and legitimate ruler. Nonetheless, the Americans themselves and others such as the French, who endorsed a philosophy like that of the Declaration, opted against monarchy and in favor of democratic republics. This, of course, is an option validated in the text, but over time the consent requirement has come to be interpreted in a much more democratic way than it is understood in the Declaration itself.

Again, we must notice that the Declaration's argument is tightly logical: The second set of truths follows deductively from the first set. The same is true and readily shown for the third set. If, as the text tells us, governments exist for a given purpose—"to secure these rights"—and if a government is instituted via consent of the governed to achieve this purpose and in no other way, then it follows that the people may withdraw their consent from governments that fail through malevolence or incompetence to achieve their purpose. Thus, the so-called right of revolution follows logically from the truths already announced. And as we have seen, the last truth follows also: So far as withdrawing consent leaves the people with no legitimate authority, they have a right to make a new government. That is, back in the condition of original equality, they have the same right, and the same need, to institute a new government.

Self-Evident Truths

We have so far passed over one of the most striking claims in the second paragraph of the Declaration: "We hold these truths to be self-evident." This claim about self-evidence has been among the most controversial features of the text. The assertion about self-evidence is often taken in modern times as evidence of the intellectual and political innocence of the simpler days of the founding.

As historian Henry Steele Commager put it, "There was indeed a simplicity in the moral standards and in political faith—a simplicity reflected ... in the language of the time: 'we hold these truths to be self-evident.'"[14] He adds later: "We would not today assume a body of 'self-evident truths,' certainly not in the arena of government or politics."[15] Sanford Levinson, political theorist and law professor, puts it even more strongly: "It is simply not open to an intellectually sophisticated modern thinker to share Jefferson's world."[16] On the other side, Danielle Allen in her study of the Declaration disagrees strongly with the self-evidence skeptics. She finds the truths affirmed in the second paragraph to be, indeed, self-evidently so and a sign of the authors' intellectual sophistication rather than the reverse.[17]

The disagreement over self-evidence is important not only as part of a contest over the American founding generation's level of intellectual development but, more importantly, for the attempt to judge the truth or falseness of the theory of government propounded in the Declaration.

This task is of preeminent importance if we are to take the Declaration as something more than a historically interesting document.

Since the Declaration as a whole constitutes one long syllogism, and since the second paragraph itself constitutes a tightly argued theory in which succeeding claims follow logically from antecedent claims, the truth value of the whole depends on our ability to affirm the truth of the initial premises. In the document as a whole, the minor premise, as provided by the long list of grievances, rests on empirical instances of kingly actions and inactions. But what does the major premise, supplied by the theoretical section, rest on? The text seems to say that these claims are self-evidently true. Their self-evidence would vouch for the truth of the theory as a whole.

Now it is apparent that these allegedly self-evident truths are not self-evident in the sense of being obvious or clearly true to all readers. The Declaration put forward a controversial theory of the origin and nature of political life; it put forward a way of looking at politics that failed to correspond to the theory and practice of nearly all nations and individuals in the world at the time. It was an innovation. Perhaps the assertion of self-evidence should be taken as not only an indication of intellectual naivete, as Commager and Levinson would argue, but also a sign of 18th-century American insularity.

To better judge the self-evidence of the claims in the Declaration demands that we reject the "obvious to everyone" interpretation of self-evidence, for the concept of self-evidence was a major theme in the philosophical literature of the age—literature in which Jefferson and others of the generation that produced the Declaration were well-versed. Particularly important is the fact that Locke, one of "the three greatest men that have ever lived, without any exception," according to Jefferson, devoted an entire chapter of his masterwork *An Essay Concerning Human Understanding* to the topic of self-evident truths.[18] Allen comes to a more favorable conclusion regarding the self-evidence and therefore truth of the Declaration's claims because she takes more seriously the philosophical meaning of self-evidence.

To judge well, one must first identify exactly what claims are identified with self-evidence. The text leaves little doubt on this score: All six truths are "held" to be self-evident. The list of six is introduced by the clause "we hold *these truths* to be self-evident," with all six standing in an exactly parallel construction, governed by that introductory clause. The text does not warrant the view, sometimes put forward, that only the first (equality) or the first two truths are held to be self-evident.

The separate and equal denomination of all the truths as held to be self-evident takes on special significance when we consult the definition of self-evident Locke put forward:

> *Knowledge* . . . consists in the perception of the agreement or disagreement of *Ideas*: Now where that agreement or disagreement is perceived immediately by it self [*sic*], without the intervention or help of any other [idea], there our *Knowledge is self-evident.*[19] (Emphasis in original.)

The most obvious example of such an immediate agreement of ideas would be a proposition of simple identity, like "*whatsoever is white is white,*" or "*Red is not Blew.*" Or a somewhat more subtle but equally self-evident proposition: "*The Whole is equal to all its Parts taken together.*"[20] (Emphasis in original.)

Several important points about the Declaration follow. Since the perception of agreement or disagreement of ideas is immediate, self-evident propositions neither require nor can depend on demonstrations or chains of reasoning of any kind.[21] A chain of reasoning, or a syllogism, involves the "intervention or help" of other ideas than those present in the original proposition. Self-evident are propositions that contain their evidence within themselves, not in their connections to other ideas. Thus, Allen is mistaken when she claims that all conclusions derived in arguments beginning with self-evident truths are themselves self-evident.[22] The bearing of this observation on the Declaration should be clear: The six truths are related to each other as steps in a deductive argument, and therefore at least the last four of them cannot be self-evident, since they are derived from other truths or ideas. But all are equally held to be self-evident. Does this mean that none is?

In fact, not one of the truths in the list of six is self-evidently true. There is no immediate agreement of ideas between the idea of man and the idea of equality as no relation of authority, in contrast to the agreement between whole and part. One can say without contradiction, as Robert Filmer did in his theory of divine right monarchy, that all men are subject to Adam and his heirs. True or false, this is not a claim that is self-evidently one or the other. Likewise, the claim that all men are endowed with the right to the pursuit of happiness is not self-evident. It may be true, but it is not self-evidently so.

As we have seen, the claim about rights serves as the first premise for the theory of legitimate government sketched in the Declaration's second paragraph, but it is not a self-evident starting point. We are entitled to ask the authors of the Declaration why they hold their claims about rights to be true, which we would be foolish to do to someone who proclaimed "red is red." All that person could do in reply is say, "Look." This would not be an appropriate answer to a query about the reasons for affirming natural rights.

So, none of the six allegedly self-evident truths is in fact self-evident. Does this mean the authors of the Declaration were ignorant, inept, or ultra-naive? To answer that question, one must look at what the text actually says. We and most students of the Declaration have been proceeding as if the text said, "These are self-evident truths." But it actually says, "*We hold* these truths to be self-evident." This is not the same. There is no room in the recognition of self-evidence for "holding." A self-evident truth is perceived directly to be such, and there is no room for a "we" who "holds" or a "holding." One way to understand or translate the "we hold" clause is to say, "We deem these truths to be self-evident." Judgments of "deeming" have no place in recognizing self-evidence.

The authors of the Declaration are therefore not claiming the actual status of self-evident truth for the six truths that together justify the

American actions but are saying something more like this: These are the basic premises for our political action. For us as a people they serve the function of self-evident truths or axioms that can serve in demonstrations. They provide the first principles for our political reasoning and acting. We are not speaking of the epistemic status of these truths but of their political status. Their epistemic status is, as Jefferson said in a letter written late in his life, a matter of the "light of science."[23]

But political communities are not composed of scientists or philosophers. One can no more expect a people to possess the philosophical ground for affirming natural rights than to grasp string theory. Political life requires that the fundamental political truths be held as deep convictions, if not as truths in the full sense. The fundamental truths must be held *as if* self-evident, as if their truth were as evident as "red is red." It is not necessary that the people as such hold the truths (or theories) of physics in this way.

Since the truths are not said to be truly self-evident, we are left wondering what argument might actually ground them. Jefferson and Locke put forth arguments for the truths, especially the primary truths of rights and equality, but not in the Declaration. This merely brings us back to an observation with which we began: The Declaration is a giving of reasons, but it is a political document, not a philosophical treatise.[24] The Declaration leads us to the threshold of political philosophy but does not go there itself.

Notes

1. See, for instance, David Armitage, *The Declaration of Independence: A Global History* (Harvard University Press, 2007); John Phillip Reid, *Constitutional History of the American Revolution: The Authority of Rights* (University of Wisconsin Press, 1986); and John Phillip Reid, "The Irrelevance of the Declaration," in *Law in the American Revolution and the Revolution in Law: A Collection of Review Essays on American Legal History*, ed. Hendrik Hartog (New York University Press, 1981).

2. Abraham Lincoln, "Gettysburg Address," speech, Gettysburg, PA, November 19, 1863, https://www.loc.gov/resource/rbpe.24404500/.

3. Danielle Allen, *Our Declaration: A Reading of the Declaration of Independence in Defense of Equality* (Liveright, 2014), 309.

4. See Pauline Maier, *American Scripture: Making the Declaration of Independence* (Vintage Books, 1998).

5. John Locke, *Two Treatises of Government* (Cambridge University Press, 1988), 269.

6. Locke, *Two Treatises of Government*.

7. Abraham Lincoln, *Speeches and Writings* (Literary Classics of the United States, 1989), 1:398.

8. See Michael Zuckert, *Launching Liberalism: On Lockean Political Philosophy* (University Press of Kansas, 2002), 220–24.

9. Zuckert, *Launching Liberalism*, 221, 274–93. See also Michael Zuckert, "Natural Rights and Imperial Constitutionalism: The American Revolution and the Development of the American Amalgam," *Social Philosophy and Policy* 22, no. 1 (2005): 27–55.

10. *Dred Scott v. Sandford*, 60 US 407 (1857).

11. Thomas Jefferson, *The Papers of Thomas Jefferson*, ed. Julian P. Boyd, vol. 1, *1760–1776* (Princeton University Press, 1950), 243–47.

12. Thomas Jefferson, *Writings* (Literary Classics of the United States, 1984), 289.

13. Jefferson, *Writings*, 1344.

14. Henry Steele Commager, *Jefferson, Nationalism, and the Enlightenment* (George Braziller, 1975), xi.

15. Commager, *Jefferson, Nationalism, and the Enlightenment*, 82.

16. Sanford Levinson, "Self-Evident Truths in the Declaration of Independence," *Texas Law Review* 57, no. 5 (1979): 856.

17. Allen, *Our Declaration*, 160–66.

18. Jefferson, *Writings*, 939; and John Locke, *An Essay Concerning Human Understanding* (1689; Oxford University Press, 1979), 591–608.

19. Locke, *An Essay Concerning Human Understanding*, 591.

20. Locke, *An Essay Concerning Human Understanding*, 596.

21. Locke, *An Essay Concerning Human Understanding*, 607–8.

22. Allen, *Our Declaration*, 16–63.

23. Jefferson, *Writings*, 1517.

24. On Jefferson, see Michael Zuckert, *The Natural Rights Republic: Studies in the Foundation of the American Political Tradition* (University of Notre Dame Press, 1996), 56–89. On Locke, see Michael Zuckert, *Natural Rights and the New Republicanism* (Princeton University Press, 1994), 275–86.

4

How the Declaration Disagrees with John Locke

DANIEL E. BURNS

When Americans in 1789 heard of France's new revolution, many assumed it was a logical successor to their own. Both revolutions seemed to be born from the same new Enlightenment-era consciousness of the universal and natural rights of man. The Declaration of the Rights of Man and of the Citizen even contained many echoes of their own Declaration of Independence. But within a few years, they were wondering, as many generations have since wondered, how the world's second natural rights revolution could have gone so poorly after the first had produced such impressive results.

We can find three very different and characteristic answers to that question in the writings of three of that period's greatest political actors. If we begin with a quick look at those three different views of the relation between the French and American Revolutions, we can better see what remains at stake today as we inquire into the meaning of the American Declaration's natural rights teaching.

Edmund Burke drew a sharper distinction between the American and French Revolutions than perhaps any other thinker of the period. He consistently supported the Americans' demands against Britain, defended their decision to declare independence, believed Britain was on the wrong side of the Revolutionary War, and insisted that he would rather have America as an independent ally than subjugate it by force.[1] This is not to say that he defended the text of our actual Declaration. The "declaration of independency" that he defends appears to be the one-line declaration of July 2—not the more memorable one of July 4, which Burke never mentioned in public.

We can infer what Burke must have thought about the Declaration's natural rights language from what he did say, in 1774–75, as the colonists increasingly justified their resistance to Great Britain by appealing to abstract principles of political right. Burke treated these appeals with benevolent condescension. He said that most citizens would never be interested in such abstract political principles unless they were provoked by some concrete grievance. In this case, that grievance was Parliament's novel and imprudent attempts to tax the Americans. So as soon as Parliament repealed all American taxes, the Americans' seeming concern for abstract principles, "born of our unhappy contest, will die along with it."[2] At the same time, Burke honored the principles that the Americans were actually acting on—because he thought they were traditional British constitutional principles, not metaphysical abstractions about the rights of man.[3]

When it came to the French, however, Burke seemed convinced that they really were acting on those metaphysical abstractions. Hence he wrote his longest book, *Reflections on the Revolution in France*, as a radical attack on not just the French Revolution but the deeper principles animating it. He even managed to predict (almost a decade before he or any Englishman knew the name of Napoléon) that, by acting on those principles, France would soon bring itself under a military dictatorship.[4]

Burke particularly objected to any attempt to confuse these newfangled, abstract, natural rights principles with the traditional British constitutional principles of the Glorious Revolution of 1688. Nearly the first quarter of his book was devoted to rebutting his countryman Richard Price, who had just published a pamphlet identifying the French revolutionary natural rights theory with the principles of their own Glorious Revolution.[5] And although Burke was too tactful to say it, Price was following there the interpretation of the Glorious Revolution originally given by John Locke. Locke had boldly asserted, in the 1689 preface to his *Two Treatises of Government*, that his own abstract natural rights theory would provide the true justification for William III's recently successful revolution. According to Burke, then, the main difference between the

American and French revolutionaries was this: Although angry Americans may sometimes have been driven to use Lockean language, only the French really acted on Lockean principles.

John Adams, a co-drafter of the Declaration, was obviously much more comfortable with its natural rights language than Burke was. Adams did not consider such language to be an attack on the traditional British constitution because he never saw any problem interpreting the British constitution in light of Lockean natural rights.[6] In fact, when Price sent Adams a personal copy of the very same pamphlet that would provoke Burke into writing the *Reflections*, Adams responded with enthusiastic praise:

> I love the zeal and the spirit which dictated this discourse, and admire the general sentiments of it. From the year 1760 to this hour, the whole scope of my life has been to support such principles and propagate such sentiments.[7]

Adams was actually concerned that the French Revolution was *insufficiently* Lockean.[8] But even more, he was deeply worried that the French, after beginning their revolution on sound Lockean natural rights principles, would fail to design a constitution that could defend those principles in practice.[9] "Locke taught them principles of liberty. But I doubt whether they have not yet to learn the principles of government."[10] In Adams's view, even Locke himself had once fallen victim to the same problem as the revolutionary French. Speaking about a real-life law code that he believed Locke to have written, Adams called it a striking example of how

> a philosopher . . . may defend the principles of liberty and the rights of mankind with great abilities and success; and, after all, when called upon to produce a plan of legislation, he may astonish the world with a signal absurdity.[11]

But, Adams promised, we could avoid such absurdities in the future. The Americans had shown the world that if a justified Lockean revolution was followed up with a well-designed constitution, it could better maintain its Lockean principles and avoid falling victim to the same corruptions that it sought to overthrow.[12] Adams's whole *Discourses on Davila* (1790) amounted to a lengthy insistence that revolutionary France's destiny was therefore now in its own hands. If France would be wise enough to form a bicameral legislature with a monarchic veto, then none of Burke's dire predictions need come true.[13] Adams thought that Napoléon's later ascendancy vindicated precisely his own criticism of French constitutional design—not any criticism of French revolutionary principles.[14]

Adams's basic view of the French Revolution—sound principles but imprudently managed—has become much more popular among Americans in the subsequent centuries, and particularly among conservatives. But for Thomas Jefferson, even this much criticism of the French Revolution was far too much. In August 1789, he wrote from France, "I will agree to be stoned as a false prophet if all does not end well in this country."[15] A month later, he famously wrote to James Madison that it was the Americans who needed to follow the French in putting their own natural rights principles more fully into practice. Under Lockean natural law, the dead cannot bind the living; hence, Jefferson tried to insist, Americans had to learn from the French and automatically abolish all their laws and public debts and constitutions every 19 years or so.[16] More than three years later, in early 1793—during the run-up to Louis XVI's execution, which Jefferson probably knew to be unjustified—Jefferson defended all the proceedings of the Jacobins, for he "considered that sect as the same with the Republican patriots" of America.[17]

> The liberty of the whole earth was depending on the issue of the contest [in France], and was ever such a prize won with so little innocent blood? My own affections have been deeply wounded by some of the martyrs to this cause, but rather than it should have failed, I would have seen half the earth desolated. Were there but an Adam & an Eve left in every country, and left free, it would be better than as it now is.[18]

Jefferson, therefore, considered any attack on the French Revolution to be an attack on the American Revolution as well. He could only see Adams's initial reservations about the French Revolution as a sign of political "apostasy" and "heresy" in his old friend. And to prevent Adams's *Discourses on Davila* from spreading that heresy, Jefferson decided to arrange the American publication of Thomas Paine's *Rights of Man*—that is, Paine's frontal attack on Burke's *Reflections on the Revolution in France*.[19] There is "no better proof" of the Americans' attachment to the "principles of republicanism" and of the American Revolution, wrote Jefferson, than that Americans "love [Paine's *Rights of Man*] and read it with delight."[20] To my knowledge, the only criticism Jefferson ever expressed of the French revolutionaries was that they were insufficiently devoted to the principle that the will of the majority stands for the will of the whole—which Jefferson, following Locke, called a "fundamental law of nature."[21]

Today, a version of Jefferson's exuberant revolutionism may still be lurking quietly in the background of much American foreign policy thinking on both the left and right.[22] But few would publicly defend his claim that the French Revolution's excesses were fully justified by American natural rights principles. At least among American conservatives of the past century, the main option seems to have been Adams or Burke.

In this chapter, I try to chart a middle course between those two very different conservative takes on the Declaration of Independence. I thus hope to bring to light aspects of the Declaration to which neither Adams's nor Burke's interpretation can do justice. For with all due deference to these great 18th-century defenders of American independence, it seems to me that both of them fail to appreciate the novelty of the American view of natural rights expressed in the Declaration of Independence. Burke goes too far by suggesting that the Americans meant *nothing* by their natural rights doctrines except that they wished not to be taxed without their consent. But Adams, too, is sloppy in equating the principles of his own American Revolution with those of Locke and the French Revolution. Adams and his fellow Americans had seen something that neither Burke nor Locke saw before them, even if Adams himself did not notice how novel it was.

To see what both Burke and Adams are missing about our Declaration, it is helpful to compare its text with Locke's *Second Treatise on Government*—particularly on the topics of natural rights, the common good, and constitutionalism. Carelessness about what Locke actually taught on these topics is pardonable in those who, like Adams, have a country to run. But for the rest of us, it is worth our time to get this comparison right. A careful look at the differences between Locke and our Declaration can help us to recognize the aspects of our own founding's distinctiveness that both Adams and Burke seem to have underappreciated. In particular, it can help us see why it is no accident that our founders managed (as Adams rightly noted) to design their state and federal constitutions so much better than the French revolutionaries. I will argue that it was the founders' distinctive, non-Lockean conception of natural rights that allowed them to do so.

Lockean Constitutionalism

The Declaration is often called a Lockean document. It obviously contains many echoes of Locke's *Second Treatise*. Yet most Americans who have heard of Locke today—and probably even at the time of the founding—have been misled by these similarities. They are unaware of how radically Locke opposed certain basic political principles that Americans since 1776 have consistently taken for granted. I will therefore begin by summarizing a few of Locke's explicit and (to Americans) surprising statements about how any legitimate government must work.

For Locke, there can be only one legislative power in any political community.[23] Locke consistently calls this the legislative "power," not the legislative "branch" as Americans prefer. For a branch is only one limb of a tree: The term implies, to this day, some degree of equality among the different and coordinate branches. Locke denies that there can be any such equality. If he had used a tree metaphor, Locke would have called the legislative power the trunk and all other governmental powers the branches and twigs.

Locke believed that the entire executive power must be entirely "derived from," and "visibly subordinate and accountable to," the legislative power. That is, the legislative has to create, appoint, delegate, hire, and fire, "at pleasure," *every single executive official*. This includes the "supream Executive Power" (i.e., chief executive) as well as the entire judiciary. (The term "executive" for Locke encompasses the judiciary.)[24] Hence when laws get executed and justice gets dispensed in courts, it is the "Legislative or Supream" power that is really taking these actions through the executive and judicial deputies to whom it gives power.[25] Those officials remain the legislative's agents, completely responsible to the legislative and only to the legislative. The same is true of "any Domestick Subordinate Power," such as provincial assemblies. These have "no manner of Authority any of them, beyond what is, by positive Grant, and Commission, delegated to them, and are all of them accountable to some other Power in the Commonwealth," namely the national legislative or one of its other deputies.[26]

Locke's legislative has, to be sure, no power to change the commonwealth's constitution. But that is because the constitution for Locke means only "the Constitution of the Legislative." It means the makeup of the legislative power, including the manner of its selection and (potentially) of its convening.[27] A Lockean constitution can say nothing about the executive and judicial branches: These must exist at the pleasure of the legislative. Nor could a Lockean constitution enumerate either the people's rights against the legislative or the limits of legislative power. Only the legislative can "decide the Rights of the Subject" and fix the "due Bounds" within which rulers must be kept.[28]

Thus for Locke, so long as a government lasts, its legislative power "must needs" be perfectly "Supream" over the whole commonwealth.[29] It is indeed as supreme as the Hobbesian sovereign, who likewise holds in his hand all executive and judicial offices as well as all subordinate legislative bodies.[30] The crucial difference from Thomas Hobbes is of course that the Lockean legislative may be fired at any time by the ultimately sovereign people, who are the only rightful judge as to whether the legislative has overstepped its inherent limits.[31] But Locke's understanding of the legislative's rights "in all Cases, whilst the Government subsists" (i.e., prior to a revolution) is still more Hobbesian than anything that almost any Patriot in 1776 could have accepted.[32]

Locke's legislative power is designed to be precisely that supreme, unchecked, ultimate political authority that the Patriots had gotten sick of hearing about from Parliament's defenders during the imperial crisis.[33] Hobbes, Locke, and many other European thinkers had insisted that such a supreme power must exist *somewhere* in any functioning government. Massachusetts Royal Governor Thomas Hutchinson even claimed that "no sensible Writer upon Government has before denied" that such a power must exist within any government.[34] Yet the rebellious Americans did deny that such a power should exist within any American government.

Hence, when Patriot pamphleteers quoted Locke during the run-up to 1776, they loved to quote his lists of the inherent limits to legislative power (including the famous no-taxation-without-representation rule). For Locke had said that the people may enforce these limits on government through their right of revolution. But the same pamphleteers consistently ignored the surrounding chapters, in which Locke explains how government is then supposed to work *after* the revolution. Had any American in 1776 commented on those chapters (and I have yet to find one who did), he would have found that they presented a familiar British view of parliamentary supremacy. In fact, he would have thought it sounded very much like the view that he and his countrymen were fighting the Revolution *against*.

The only contemporary pamphleteer whom I have found quoting any of the above-cited passages from Locke is the anti-American British bureaucrat William Knox. Knox, of course, uses those Lockean passages to defend Lockean parliamentary supremacy, which he applies against the authority of the colonial legislatures.[35] Meanwhile, the only American revolutionary who may have been sympathetic to these views of Locke's seems to be Paine. For Paine's *Common Sense* demanded first an American revolution, but then also a new supreme national American legislature. America needed a "continental form of government," said Paine, with all 13 state legislatures made "subject to the authority of a Continental Congress," whose members would be "the legislators and governors of this continent" while in office, with apparently no other branches of government appointed to check them.[36] Americans responded to Paine's call for revolution. They completely ignored his call for a new and fully supreme national legislature.

To get a sense of how little the Americans of 1776 cared about Locke's actual political philosophy, we can look at the two pre-1776 American pamphlets that include (so far as I know) the most extensive quotations from England's most quotable Whig philosopher. James Otis's opening salvo of the imperial crisis (1764), as well as the famous "Boston Pamphlet" drafted by Samuel Adams and others (1772), both contain long block quotes from Locke's *Second Treatise* on the limits of the legislative power. Yet in both cases, these quotations get significantly doctored by the respective pamphlet authors. And neither gives any indication of knowing (or caring) that he is changing Locke's meaning—much less that these changes are flatly contradicted by Locke's statements just a few pages later in the *Second Treatise*.

Thus, faced with Locke's claim that only the legislature can "decide the Rights of the Subject," Otis simply deletes the phrase from his quotation from Locke. The Bostonians instead alter the grammar so that the legislature is no longer the one deciding. Both Otis and the Bostonians boldly insert the word "independent" before Locke's word "judges." Where Locke had said that the legislature is "bound to dispense justice" through its subordinate judges, the Bostonians alter it so that the legislature is only "bound to see that justice is dispensed" by independent judges.[37] And when quoting Locke on the supreme legislative power, Otis brazenly inserts the un-Lockean and pro-American claims that "subordinate legislative" bodies have rights against the "supreme" national legislative body and that those subordinate legislative bodies are constituted independently by "the community" (rather than by a supreme legislative authority that can fire them again at pleasure).[38]

Any one of these would have been a career-ending act of dishonesty if Otis or the Bostonians had been engaged in academic scholarship on

Locke. But they did not claim to be. I would be surprised if either had intended to mislead their readers. My best guess is that both believed, erroneously, that they were simply offering friendly amendments to correct lapses or infelicities of expression by the great Whig philosopher and defender (as they assumed) of the post-1688 British constitution. The same assumption about Locke was likely made by most, or even all, of the other Revolutionary-era Americans whom these pamphlet authors represented and influenced. Even among Americans who read Locke today, I have generally found the same lack of interest in his manifest disagreements with American understandings of constitutionalism. When confronted with those disagreements, Americans tend to respond with a shrug that says, "Too bad for Locke."

I do not think we can leave it at that shrug if we wish to understand the Declaration of Independence correctly. For Locke was at least as suspicious of arbitrary, unchecked power as any Patriot in 1776. If he believed that so much unchecked power had to be granted to the legislative in any government, he must have had a reason for believing so. What was his reason?

Lockean Natural Rights and the Common Good

Locke believed he had no choice. His constitutionalism, such as it is, follows directly and logically from his understanding of the purpose of government. And his understanding of the purpose of government, in turn, follows directly from his famous teaching on the state of nature and natural rights. Americans were able to disagree with Locke's constitutionalism only because they already disagreed with his understanding of natural rights.

According to Locke, natural law commands no more and no less than the comfortable, bodily preservation of all mankind.[39] This is the same as saying that it commands the preservation of everyone's natural rights to life (including health), bodily liberty, and property. For liberty and property are "means of" comfortable self-preservation and are, under Lockean natural law, valued only as such.[40] This same natural law sets the strict limits of all governmental power. Political society is formed precisely when naturally free individuals hand over to society their own power of enforcing this same natural law.[41] The political society formed in this manner—and a fortiori its legislative, whose powers are merely delegated by the society—can therefore have no power except what is needed to preserve life, liberty, and property. The legislative power can never "destroy, enslave, or . . . designedly impoverish" its subjects in the service of any cause whatsoever.[42] Locke makes that assertion, and then he restates it: The legislative power "is limited to the publick good of the Society" or must serve "the good of the People."[43] In other words, since the Lockean political common good is defined by the Lockean natural rights teaching, "the common good" in Lockean political society is limited to the preservation of "every one"—that is, "himself his Liberty and Property."[44]

War, for Locke, is a state of "Mutual Destruction" and hence the polar opposite of mutual preservation. This is why Locke can also say that natural law commands "the Peace and Preservation of all Mankind."[45] Hence, "one great reason" why people form governments is to avoid the state of war.[46] Locke understands the state of war roughly as Hobbes understood it: a lawless, amoral fight to the death, where neither side is bound by any rules or rights except the rational desire to escape the state of war where possible.[47] Locke famously insists that our natural state is, *pace* Hobbes, a state of peace.[48] But he is equally clear that in that natural state of peace, "every the least difference is apt to end" in the Hobbesian state of war.[49] For in a state of peace without government to protect us, everyone still has the natural right to regard the slightest perceived threat to his life, liberty, or property—indeed, "reason bids me look on" any such threat—as a plunge into the state of war.[50]

For this reason, Locke considers it an essential and nonnegotiable task of government to prevent any and all of the threats that could reintroduce the very state of war that civil society is designed to prevent. Government therefore has to resolve "every the least difference," to the extent it can. Humans under government must never be allowed to risk a fight by laying claim to the same property. Government *must* exclude "*all* private judgement of every particular Member," and must decide "*all* the differences that may happen between *any* Members of that Society, concerning *any* matter of right."[51] (Emphasis added.) If your so-called government includes no "known Authority, to which *every one* of that Society may Appeal upon *any* Injury received, or Controversie that may arise," then you have no government at all, and your would-be citizens are "still in the state of nature."[52] (Emphasis added.) For a government that fails to reliably protect our natural rights actually leaves us worse off than in the state of nature, and so would not receive the consent of any rational human.[53]

Thus, Locke leaves no place for any government official to claim that a particular act of the legislative power is invalid—so long as this legislative power remains in place (that is, in a situation short of revolution). In fact, Locke deliberately designs his political system to rule out any such claim. Because a single and ultimate authority must be able to "determine all the Controversies . . . that may happen to any Member of the Commonwealth," this single and ultimate authority can only be the legislative or the magistrates it appoints (and can replace) at pleasure.[54] For if a chief executive, any number of high-court judges, or an entire provincial legislature could challenge a procedurally valid law passed by a valid national legislative power, then we would have on our hands a controversy with no governmental authority to resolve it. This would be true even if the law were being challenged by an appeal to some written constitution that the law allegedly contradicts. For who would have the constitutional power to interpret this written constitution? If the legislative has such a power, then it can simply reinterpret the constitution to resolve the conflict in its own favor. But if instead someone else were the final judge of the legislative power's limits, then that inferior official could override some of its acts while the rest remained in place. Locke calls that idea "ridiculous" and even "impossible to conceive."[55] For it would leave it ultimately unclear to ordinary citizens what is "*the* Standard of Right and Wrong . . . to decide *all* Controversies" between them, and hence it would leave them open to the type of ambiguity that can lead to disagreement, conflict, an appeal to force, and eventually civil war.[56] (Emphasis added.)

Locke's constitutionalism follows from his natural rights teaching. Like Hobbes, he regards civil war as the *summum malum* of all political life, since it is the greatest of all risks to our fundamental natural right of comfortable preservation.[57] A political system would be irrational, and hence impossible for rational creatures to consent to, if it permitted that risk to exist anywhere that it had the option of eliminating it—at whatever cost. No other consideration, no real or alleged common good could possibly be balanced against the risk of avoidable, violent conflict. The government has no business caring about any real or alleged good other than comfortable bodily preservation.

The American Founders' Un-Lockean Constitutionalism

At this point it should be clear how foreign to American political thought is Lockean constitutionalism. From 1788 on, we have taken for granted that we should have an independent executive, an independent judiciary, state governments with their own independent authority not delegated from Congress, and enumerated constitutional rights that limit the legislative power itself. All these standard features of American constitutionalism are not only absent from Locke's thought but expressly contradicted by it. Had our federal Constitution been written by convinced Lockeans, it would have ended at Article I, Section 7.

Nor is this an instance in which the period 1787–88 produced some radical improvements unthought of in 1776. Every state constitution, written in 1776 and thereafter, already presupposes that the people of each state constitute its executive and judicial branches in addition to its legislative branch. Every state constitution presupposes that those other branches can act as independent checks on the legislative—not only as its deputies. (In Washington's 1787 letter to Congress introducing the new federal constitution, he states as an obvious deduction that, once we needed to give Congress new legislative powers, we would also need to constitute two other branches of government to check Congress.)[58] Every state constitution also presupposes that the people can, and indeed ought to, enumerate positive restrictions on the legislative power in the form of bills of rights. Those rights included not only natural rights but positive civil rights (such as trial by jury). The people of each state thought they were, by writing these constitutions, putting these enumerated rights out of the reach of their own legislative branches.

And many American political thinkers before *Marbury v. Madison*—starting with Otis in 1764—argued that the judicial branch could and should enforce these same positive, constitutional rights against the legislative branch.[59] They did not agree with Locke that the people can vindicate their civil rights against the legislature only by the extreme expedient of a revolution. When Americans from the 1760s onward have used the word "constitution," they have consistently referred to something that Locke thought impossible. John Dickinson in 1767—just before quoting Locke on the principle of no taxation without consent—defines "a free people" as "*those*, who live under a government so *constitutionally checked and controuled*, that proper provision is made against its being" exercised unreasonably.[60] (Emphasis in original.) The Bostonian preacher John Tucker, in 1771, cites the Lockean state-of-nature teaching, but concludes from it that

> the fundamental laws, which . . . form the political constitution of the state,—which mark out, and fix the chief lines and boundaries between the authority of Rulers, and the liberties and privileges of the people, are, and can be no other, in a free state, than what are mutually agreed upon and consented to.

He goes on to say that only these "constitutional laws of the state," and no mere governmental authority, "are, properly, the supreme power, being obligatory on the whole community," including on the legislature itself.[61]

The Town of Boston, in 1772, asserts with Locke that "when Men enter into Society, it is by voluntary Consent." From this they, too, conclude that such men must "have a Right to demand and insist upon the Performance [by their legislature] of such Conditions and previous Limitations as form an equitable *original Compact*."[62] (Emphasis in original.)

An anonymous but popular Philadelphia pamphlet in 1776 follows the same logic:

> Individuals ... agreeing to erect forms of government ... must give up some part of their liberty for that purpose; and it is the particular business of a Constitution to make out *how much* they shall give up, [saying] to the legislative powers, "Thus far shalt thou go, and no farther."[63] (Emphasis in original.)

In light of British parliamentary supremacy, the pamphlet argues, the British in reality have no constitution.

The loyalist Charles Inglis, in 1776, defines "constitution" as "*that assemblage of laws, customs and institutions which form the general system; according to which the several powers of the state are distributed, and their respective rights are secured to the different members of the community.*"[64] (Emphasis in original.) The "Essex Result" of 1778 expects a constitution to establish "the several lines in which the various powers of government are to move," which require the people's positive civil rights to be "ascertained and defined ... with a precision sufficient to limit the legislative power." It again derives this expectation from a seemingly Lockean state-of-nature teaching.[65] Even Paine, in his swiftly ignored demand for a national supreme legislative power, still seems to assume that the expected "Continental Charter" (a national written constitution) should delineate "the line of business and jurisdiction between" Congress and the state legislatures and should include a bill of rights. Even Paine assumes that these restrictions on the legislative power belong to "such ... matter as is necessary for a charter to contain."[66]

Americans thus rejected Lockean constitutionalism from the beginning. And we have seen that Lockean constitutionalism is closely connected to Lockean natural rights. It therefore seems to me that the Declaration of Independence's apparently small deviations from the Lockean natural rights teaching are more significant than is usually noted.

The American Founders on Natural Rights and the Common Good

As we saw above, it is essential to Locke's political teaching that our *only* natural right is to comfortable self-preservation—that is, to life, health, liberty, and property. Locke is often associated as well with the so-called rights of conscience (a phrase he never uses in his published writings), but those rights are epiphenomenal on his view. Locke thinks we have a natural right not to follow the dictates of our own conscience but to live under a government that is concerned only with preserving the genuine rights of life, liberty, and property—a government that will interfere with our religion only insofar as our religion interferes with the government's attempts to preserve life, liberty, and property.[67]

The Declaration of Independence refuses to limit our natural rights as Locke did. It lists only three natural rights, but it says these are among *other*, unnamed natural rights. And one of the three rights that it does name is the ambiguous, and potentially expansive, "pursuit of Happiness." This, too, is a Lockean phrase, but it appears in Locke's treatise on psychology, not on politics—and for good reason.[68] For as Locke emphasizes there, the pursuit of happiness means all sorts of things to all sorts of people.[69] Such a polysemous right could never be a basis for the peaceful and conflict-averse Lockean society, which must agree on uniform regulations for the unambiguous, natural goods of life, liberty, and property.[70]

The Declaration's more expansive understanding of natural rights is visible in every reference to natural rights that I have seen in official founding-era documents. That is, unlike the French Declaration of the Rights of Man and of the Citizen, every public founding-era American enumeration of natural rights explicitly says that these rights go somehow beyond the Lockean rights of comfortable self-preservation. (I am taking for granted that none of the founders—particularly none of those who mutually pledged "our Lives, our Fortunes and our sacred Honor" to the fight against tyranny—regarded the pursuit of happiness as definitionally identical or reducible to "property" or "comfortable self-preservation.")

It is to secure *these* natural rights—including the non-Lockean right to the pursuit of happiness and others not listed—that the Declaration says governments "are instituted among men." Thus, when the founders stated the truism that governments ought to protect the common good, they did not understand that common good as reducible to comfortable self-preservation or to life, liberty, and property. Naturally, they wanted their governments to secure life, liberty, and property (as did every political thinker prior to Karl Marx). But it is no secret that they also wanted their governments to secure other common goods.

I will name just a few examples of those goods, as the founders saw them:

- Public morality;

- Moral education of the young;

- Intellectual education of the young;

- Sabbath rest;

- A healthy marriage culture;

- Worship of God according to the dictates of each person's conscience, but also sometimes communally;

- Republican self-government, including jury trials and full civic participation by all property owners (not just the Lockean right to vote on tax increases);[71] and

- The rule of law—understood as a law above all individuals and groups, binding even on the popularly elected legislative power, and even (as far as republican principles will permit) binding on the majority of the people themselves.

According to the Declaration's logic, the founders may have thought that these other, non-Lockean political goods belonged among our other, unnamed natural rights. Or they may have thought that these other political goods were components of the pursuit of happiness. Or they may have thought both. Certainly none of them ever claimed that all the other common goods listed above were simply means to the protection of life, liberty, and property. I am not aware of any founder who, for instance, felt the need to argue publicly, as Locke was forced to argue, that the reason "Adultery, Incest and Sodomy" should be criminalized is that they impede population growth.[72] Rather, the founders were satisfied with the following type of deduction: Good public schools are needed because "religion, morality and knowledge" are "necessary to good government *and* the happiness of mankind."[73] (Emphasis added.)

The founders' understanding of natural rights was capacious enough to encompass what they believed mattered most in human life. It encompassed what they believed they knew about how humans pursue happiness, as it had been taught to them by the institutions that formed their souls: their families, their schools, and their churches. The language of the Declaration, one could say, incorporates by reference what the founders had learned from those institutions. Today, we have undergone a different formation, so we will interpret in the Declaration's terse formulas a somewhat different list of political common goods—although I hope not radically different.

Either way, any conception of the common good grounded in the Declaration of Independence will be more expansive than the Lockean conception. It will therefore be in some tension with the Lockean conception. Locke saw this as clearly as anyone, which is why comparing him to the founders is so helpful here. One cannot have a government instituted to secure non-Lockean common goods without some risk to the Lockean common goods. Hence Locke thought that governments had to confine themselves to securing the Lockean common goods. Yet because of the founders' more expansive conception of natural rights and the common good, they went so far as to enshrine non-Lockean aspects of the political common good in their state constitutions, and even—to a more limited degree, given its limited scope—in their federal constitution. They bound their legislatures in writing to secure *these* rights, even though that would mean some unavoidable trade-offs for comfortable self-preservation. And even where they did not specifically mention non-Lockean rights or goods in their constitutions, they simply took for granted that state and federal legislatures would pass laws securing those non-Lockean rights and goods. They never dreamed that their judiciary would invalidate such laws as contrary to the legitimate purposes of government (the way Locke suggests it should).[74]

Perhaps the most important of these non-Lockean common goods pursued by our founding-era governments was the rule of law in its more-than-Lockean sense. For to ensure the rule of law rather than men, the founders consciously refused to create in any of their constitutions a single, ultimate governmental power with unambiguous authority to judge any potential disputes between private individuals or public officials.

Instead, they divided power among the three branches of government. They did this first at the state level and then, once it became clear that an actual federal legislative power was needed, again at the federal level. They made the executive independent of the legislature. They armed the executive in most states and at the federal level with the legislative veto to defend its independence. They made judges likewise independent of the legislature, choosing them either by election or by executive appointment. They armed federal and some state judges with the extra protection of lifetime tenure. They allowed those judges to enforce *positive* constitutional provisions (not the Lockean natural law) against the legislature. They built up a body of what we now call "constitutional law," which not even the legislature can change and which, therefore, contains permanent potential for conflict and ambiguity over "the Standard of Right and Wrong," "the Rights of the Subject," and the "due Bounds" of rulers.[75] Perhaps most significantly, the founders soon invented a remarkable and historically unprecedented type of constitutionalism, under which the supreme government would have only enumerated powers, while the subordinate governments retained sovereign power in their proper spheres. I have not heard of a single American in the subsequent 236 years expressing the Lockean view that the residual sovereignty of states, as "Domestick Subordinate Powers," must have been delegated to them by the United States Congress.[76]

Of course, not all of this American non-Lockean constitutionalism was yet fully clear in the minds of the signers of the Declaration of Independence. But some of its aspects, such as the separation of coordinate branches of government, were already clear to them. We can gather this from how quickly after July 1776 the Declaration's signers went home and wrote state constitutions that enshrined that separation. Other aspects of American constitutionalism, especially federalism and—to some extent—judicial review, would develop over the coming decade or two. But the Declaration is already visibly open to those developments. Locke could never have been open to an arrangement where the Supreme Court could overturn some laws, Congress could pass new laws if it wanted to, and the executive branch could reinterpret those laws if it wanted to—where no single power has the unambiguous right to bind the actions of all Americans in case of serious disagreement.

Today, when we read the clauses in which the Declaration of Independence signals its openness to our subsequent constitutionalism, we take their views so much for granted that we may miss how important and controversial they are. Again, we can understand these clauses better by contrasting them with Lockean thought. Here are those familiar clauses: "laying its foundation on such principles, and organizing its powers in such form, as to them shall seem most likely to effect their Safety and Happiness."

Locke thought he had already set out in his *Treatises* the principles on which the foundations of every valid government must be laid. He left no room for the people to lay their foundation on whatever principles may seem to them most likely to effect their own happiness, particularly if this "happiness" is defined as anything beyond comfortable self-preservation.

Likewise, Locke thought he had already set out how any government's powers have to be organized: The legislative must be absolutely supreme, and all other powers will be organized however the legislative wants to organize them. Locke knew his views were unusual. Many countries of his day had what they regarded as set "Constitutions," specifying how various of their nonlegislative powers should be organized.[77] But as we have seen, Locke was confident that this was not the rational meaning of "constitution," which can only mean the makeup of the supreme legislative power. Finally, Locke thought that the people constituted that legislative power only to ensure their "comfortable, safe, and peaceable living," not their safety and happiness.[78] Or rather, he thought the people constituted their legislative to ensure such "Political Happiness" as can be ensured by a government that, aiming only at the Lockean common good of comfortable preservation, must and will sacrifice all other considerations in order to secure *that* common good.[79]

The Declaration is probably again referring to the Americans' non-Lockean constitutionalism in its lapidary phrase "Deriving their just powers from the consent of the governed." For the most natural way to read that phrase is that different valid governments may have *different* just powers, depending on what the governed have chosen to consent to.[80] At least this is what nearly all Americans, both at the time and since, appear to have assumed. For only on that reading would it be important for us to write down positive, constitutional enumerations of the precise governmental powers that we have (and have not) consented to. According to Locke (and Hobbes), by contrast, all valid governments everywhere have exactly the same powers by consent of the governed.[81] On that view, any written constitutions would at least have been much shorter and less necessary than on the usual American view. All subsequent American constitutionalism thus rests on what Locke, in light of his own natural rights teaching, believed to be a logical impossibility.

At any rate, the Declaration of Independence asserts that our natural rights give us the political right to choose principles of government—and organize its powers—with a view to political happiness as we collectively understand it. That is, our natural rights give us the political right to write our constitutions as we see fit, just as the American states quickly began to do in 1776. That political right is indeed what the Declaration is most immediately defending. Its preamble would never have mentioned natural rights unless its authors were convinced that natural rights, correctly understood, are the foundation of the political right to write our own constitutions as we see fit. Yet according to Locke, if we correctly understand natural rights, we should see that nobody ever has the political right to write the sort of constitutions that Americans wanted to write.

Locke denies the political premise of American constitutionalism because he is confident that, as rational creatures, we could never rationally assent to any avoidable risk to our own natural right to bodily self-preservation—nor, therefore, to a government that would pursue any common good other than bodily self-preservation. American constitutionalism presupposes the Declaration's understanding of natural rights and the common good rather than Locke's.

In particular, because of their understanding of the rule of law, the founders created a constitutional division of limited powers among different branches with no governmental authority entirely supreme over any other. They were aware (to at least some extent) that the rule of law in this sense would mean risking a constitutional crisis unresolvable by the text of the Constitution itself, and hence risking civil war.[82] They chose to form no Leviathan, no unstoppable earthly power to prevent that civil war. At some point, the only power to prevent such a war would be their own awareness of the sacred bonds that united them to each other as fellow Americans.[83] The risk still did not appear to them intolerable.

In light of all that we have seen from Locke, this might mean that the founders departed from his thought in one of two ways. Maybe they did not share Locke's Hobbesian terror of civil war as the absolute *summum malum* in this life. Or maybe they did not share Locke's Hobbesian optimism that human beings, guided by rational political philosophy, can construct a government that will permanently rule out the danger of that civil war.[84] Or, more likely as it seems to me, they shared neither view. The founders were afraid of violent death, but they were also afraid of other things. And they knew that if governments are to have any chance of securing *all* the rights for the sake of which they are instituted among men, then governments cannot be constantly hemmed in by the political maxim that is the ultimate consequence of the Hobbesian and Lockean natural rights doctrines: "Safety first."

A Novel Natural Rights Teaching

Adams was thus wrong to think that he and the French revolutionaries were all animated by the same Lockean natural rights principles. As Locke proves so elegantly, our understanding of natural rights determines our understanding of the proper ends of government, which in turn determines the limits of what we can do when writing a political constitution. The Americans could write the constitutions that they did only because they had already departed significantly from the Lockean natural rights teaching. If Adams did not read Locke carefully enough to notice these departures, then the oversight, at any rate, seems to have done little harm to Adams's own drafting of the Massachusetts Constitution. (His biggest innovation in that constitution, the qualified executive veto, would soon be copied into our federal Constitution as the mainstay of its anti-Lockean executive independence.)[85]

Conversely, although it would take much more work to prove Burke's assertion that the defects of the French revolutionaries' constitution followed directly from the defects in their understanding of natural rights, that assertion appears highly plausible in light of what we have seen.[86] Burke himself offered an alternative and more moderate understanding of natural rights.[87] But Burke, too, failed to understand what the American colonists meant by those rights. The Declaration's rage at King George arose from Americans' long-frustrated hopes that their beloved king would assert his executive independence and check Parliament's tyrannical depredations on their subordinate legislatures' rightful authority.[88] Americans were rejecting with contempt, and in large numbers, the 1766 Declaratory Act's assertion of absolute parliamentary supremacy.

Burke, by contrast, voted for the Declaratory Act in Parliament and supported it right up until its repeal in 1778.[89] He had read the philosophically grounded American protests against parliamentary supremacy but, as he said, "I do not enter into these metaphysical distinctions; I hate the very sound of them" and he "never ventured to put [Parliament's] solid interests upon speculative grounds."[90] He believed, mistakenly, that the real American grievances could be fully resolved by prudent and statesmanly action from a still-supreme and uncheckable Parliament.

It is not enough to note that, as shown by Burke's repeated failures from 1767 through 1778, his colleagues in Parliament were incapable of that prudent and statesmanly action. For even before Lexington and Concord, the most farsighted Americans were already demanding what Burke thought impossible: written, constitutional checks on the authority of Parliament to legislate for its colonies, checks that would bind Parliament itself.[91] Not until the Revolutionary War had begun did Burke reluctantly acknowledge that the British Empire would need to invent constitutional checks of this kind, and even then, he could imagine no power higher than Parliament to enforce them.[92] The Americans had sensed, before even the wise Burke, that a new kind of written constitution would be needed to bind both the national and the subordinate legislatures of a modern federal empire under the rule of law. And in the American mind, the demand for such a constitution was a direct consequence of their own understanding of natural rights and the common good.

Burke and Locke had two very different understandings of natural rights—different from the Americans' and even more different from each other. Yet remarkably, those different understandings still led them by different paths toward accepting, in their respective ways, the old British view of national legislative supremacy. If Parliament had just given the Americans the right to vote on tax increases, then Burke and Locke could each have been satisfied. By 1776, the Americans could not be.

The Declaration of Independence arose out of, and gives voice to, the Americans' rejection of the old British view of national legislative supremacy. Its wording clearly reflects that origin. The American political commonplaces that it expresses so beautifully would become, 12 years later, the basis for the American people's most astonishing political success. For in 1788 and thereafter, Americans would succeed where Burke and his parliamentary colleagues had failed: They would build a modern federal empire of free governments under the rule of law.

The founders' deviations from the Lockean natural rights teaching are therefore essential to their political thought and their political success. What may seem like small verbal deviations from Locke—"among these are," "the pursuit of Happiness"—reflect substantive changes with truly massive constitutional consequences. Without those departures from Lockean thought on natural rights and the common good, the United States as we know it would never have gotten off the ground. Even and precisely if Americans could have allowed Paine to actualize here his Lockean fantasy of a national supreme legislature (as it was briefly actualized in France), we would likely never have made it to 1787, let alone 2026.

Conservatives, in particular, have long been tempted to invoke Locke against his socialist adversaries. This may have been pardonable during the Cold War. But we will need to look to other intellectual sources if we wish to understand and defend the constitutional, legal, and moral structures that have truly made our country what it is. Those structures include our peculiar, homegrown understanding of natural rights. We can see as much in the Declaration's own remarkably lucid text—particularly when we read it alongside the equally clear statements by Locke that contradict it.

Notes

1. "Speech on American Taxation," in *The Writings and Speeches of Edmund Burke*, ed. Paul Langford, vol. 2, *Party, Parliament, and the American Crisis, 1766–1774*, ed. William B. Todd (Clarendon Press, 1981), 406–63; "Speech on Conciliation with America, 11 March 1775," in *The Writings and Speeches of Edmund Burke*, ed. Paul Langford, vol. 3,

Party, Parliament, and the American War, 1774–1780, ed. Warren M. Elofson and John A. Woods (Clarendon Press, 1996), 102–69; "Second Speech on Conciliation, 17 Nov 1775," in *The Writings and Speeches of Edmund Burke*, 3:183–220; "Speech on Cavendish's Motion on America, 6 Nov 1776," in *The Writings and Speeches of Edmund Burke*, 3:253; "Address to the King [Jan 1777]," in *The Writings and Speeches of Edmund Burke*, 3:264, 269; "Address to the Colonists [Jan 1777]," in *The Writings and Speeches of Edmund Burke*, 3:279, 283–84; and "Speech on the Use of Indians, 6 Feb 1778," in *The Writings and Speeches of Edmund Burke*, 3:364.

2. "Speech on American Taxation," in *The Writings and Speeches of Edmund Burke*, 2:458; "Speech on Conciliation with America," in *The Writings and Speeches of Edmund Burke*, 3:138–39, 146; "Second Speech on Conciliation," in *The Writings and Speeches of Edmund Burke*, 3:196; and "Letter to the Sheriffs of Bristol, 3 April 1777," in *The Writings and Speeches of Edmund Burke*, 3:318–19.

3. "Amendment to Address, 31 Oct 1776," in *The Writings and Speeches of Edmund Burke*, 3:251; "Petition for Bristol [Jan 1777]," in *The Writings and Speeches of Edmund Burke*, 3:257; and "Letter to the Sheriffs of Bristol," in *The Writings and Speeches of Edmund Burke*, 3:329.

4. Edmund Burke, *Reflections on the Revolution in France* (1790; Stanford University Press, 2002), 387–88.

5. Burke, *Reflections on the Revolution in France*, 155–231.

6. "A Dissertation on the Canon and the Feudal Law," in *The Works of John Adams, Second President of the United States: With a Life of the Author, Notes and Illustrations, by His Grandson Charles Francis Adams*, ed. Charles Francis Adams, vol. 3 (Little, Brown, 1851), 461, 456–57.

7. John Adams to Richard Price, 19 April 1790, in *The Works of John Adams, Second President of the United States*, 9:563.

8. John Adams to Richard Price, 19 April 1790, in *The Works of John Adams, Second President of the United States*, 9:563–64.

9. John Adams to Richard Price, 19 April 1790, in *The Works of John Adams, Second President of the United States*, 9:564.

10. John Adams to Samuel Adams, 12 September 1790, in *The Works of John Adams, Second President of the United States*, 6:411–12.

11. Adams assumes erroneously that Locke had a free hand in the drafting of the Fundamental Constitutions of Carolina. "A Defence of the Constitutions of Government of the United States of America, Against the Attack of M. Turgot, in His Letter to Dr. Price, Dated the Twenty-Second Day of March, 1778, vol. 1," in *The Works of John Adams, Second President of the United States*, 4:463.

12. "A Defence of the Constitutions of Government of the United States of America, Against the Attack of M. Turgot, in His Letter to Dr. Price, Dated the Twenty-Second Day of March, 1778, vol. 1," in *The Works of John Adams, Second President of the United States*, 4:284, 289–91, 296–98.

13. *Discourses on Davila*, in *The Works of John Adams, Second President of the United States*, 6:252, 273–74, 284, 299–300, 323, 340–41, 365, 399.

14. *Discourses on Davila*, in *The Works of John Adams, Second President of the United States* 6:274n, 299n, 300n, 312n, 393n, 394nn.

15. Thomas Jefferson to Diodati, August 3, 1789, in *Thomas Jefferson, Writings: Autobiography, Notes on the State of Virginia, Public and Private Papers, Addresses, Letters*, ed. Merrill Peterson (Library of America, 1984), 958.

16. Thomas Jefferson to James Madison, September 6, 1789, in *Thomas Jefferson: Writings*, 959–64. The Lockean statement is "that whatever Engagements or Promises any one has made for himself, he is under the Obligation of them, but cannot by any Compact whatsoever, bind his Children or Posterity." John Locke, *Two Treatises of Government* (1689; Cambridge University, 1970), 2.116.

17. Jefferson calls Louis XVI an "honest," "unambitious" king, selflessly devoted to his people's welfare in Thomas Jefferson to John Jay, May 9, 1789, in *Thomas Jefferson: Writings*, 952–53.

18. Jefferson to William Short, January 3, 1793, in *Thomas Jefferson: Writings*, 1004.

19. "To the President of the United States (George Washington)," May 8, 1791, in *Thomas Jefferson: Writings*, 977–78.

20. Thomas Jefferson to Thomas Paine, June 19, 1792, in *Thomas Jefferson: Writings*, 992.

21. Thomas Jefferson to John Breckinridge, January 29, 1800, in *Thomas Jefferson: Writings*, 1074. For Locke's statement of this "Law of Nature and Reason," see John Locke, *Two Treatises of Government*, 2.95–99.

22. Daniel E. Burns, "An Arab Spring Autopsy," *The American Interest*, July–August 2018, 43–47, https://www.the-american-interest.com/2018/04/05/arab-spring-autopsy/.

23. Locke, *Two Treatises of Government*, 2.132, 2.143.

24. Locke, *Two Treatises of Government*, 2.150–53. See also the definitions of "executive" in Locke, *Two Treatises of Government*, 2.88, 2.147.

25. Locke, *Two Treatises of Government*, 2.131, 2.136, 2.150.

26. Locke, *Two Treatises of Government*, 2.134, 2.152.

27. Locke, *Two Treatises of Government*, 2.153–57, 2.132.

28. Locke, *Two Treatises of Government*, 2.136, 2.137.

29. Locke, *Two Treatises of Government*, 2.150.

30. Thomas Hobbes, *Leviathan* (1651; Hackett, 1994), 110–18.

31. Locke, *Two Treatises of Government*, 2.149, 2.240.

32. Locke, *Two Treatises of Government*, 2.150.

33. "To the Inhabitants of Great Britain," in *The Papers of James Iredell*, ed. Don Higginbotham, vol. 1, 1767–1777 (North Carolina Department of Cultural Resources, 1976), 263–65.

34. Thomas Hutchinson, "The Speeches of His Excellency Governor Hutchinson, to the General Assembly of the Massachusetts-Bay," in *The American Revolution: Writings from the Pamphlet Debate*, ed. Gordon S. Wood, vol. 2, 1773–1776 (Library of America, 2015), 77.

35. William Knox, "The Controversy Between Great Britain and Her Colonies Reviewed," in *The American Revolution: Writings from the Pamphlet Debate*, ed. Gordon S. Wood, vol. 1, 1764–1772 (Library of America, 2015), 647.

36. Thomas Paine, *Common Sense; Addressed to the Inhabitants of America*, in Wood, *The American Revolution*, 2:677–79.

37. James Otis, "The Rights of the British Colonies Asserted and Proved," in Wood, *The American Revolution*, 1:77; Town of Boston, "The Votes and Proceedings, in Town Meeting Assembled, According to Law," in Wood, *The American Revolution*, 1:768; and Locke, *Two Treatises of Government*, 2.136.

38. Otis, "The Rights of the British Colonies Asserted and Proved," 75; and Locke, *Two Treatises of Government*, 2.134.

39. Locke, *Two Treatises of Government*, 2.6, 2.135, 2.183. For the assumption that "preservation" means "comfortable preservation," see Locke, *Two Treatises of Government*, 1.86–87, 2.95.

40. Locke, *Two Treatises of Government*, 2.149.
41. Locke, *Two Treatises of Government*, 2.87–89.
42. Locke, *Two Treatises of Government*, 2.135.
43. Locke, *Two Treatises of Government*, 2.135, 2.142.
44. Locke, *Two Treatises of Government*, 2.131, 2.135.
45. Locke, *Two Treatises of Government*, 2.19, 2.7, 2.8.
46. Locke, *Two Treatises of Government*, 2.21.
47. Locke, *Two Treatises of Government*, 2.16–24; and Hobbes, *Leviathan*, 76.
48. Locke, *Two Treatises of Government*, 2.19.
49. Locke, *Two Treatises of Government*, 2.21.
50. Locke, *Two Treatises of Government*, 2.16–18.
51. Locke, *Two Treatises of Government*, 2.87.
52. Locke, *Two Treatises of Government*, 2.89–90.
53. Locke, *Two Treatises of Government*, 2.90–94, 2.137.
54. Locke, *Two Treatises of Government*, 2.89.
55. Locke, *Two Treatises of Government*, 2.132, 2.134, 2.150.
56. Locke, *Two Treatises of Government*, 2.124.
57. Locke, *Two Treatises of Government*, 2.230; and Hobbes, *Leviathan*, 219.

58. George Washington, "Letter to the President of Congress," in *George Washington: Writings*, ed. John H. Rhodehamel (Library of America, 1997), 654.

59. Otis, "The Rights of the British Colonies," 81, 87; *Federalist*, no. 16 (Hamilton); *Federalist*, no. 33 (Hamilton); *Federalist*, no. 39 (Madison); *Federalist*, no. 42 (Madison); and Thomas Jefferson to James Madison, March 15, 1789, in *Thomas Jefferson: Writings*, 943.

60. John Dickinson, "Letters from a Farmer in Pennsylvania, to the Inhabitants of the British Colonies," in Wood, *The American Revolution*, 1:449–50.

61. John Tucker, "An Election Sermon," in *American Political Writing During the Founding Era, 1760–1805*, ed. Charles S. Hyneman and Donald S. Lutz (Liberty Fund, 1983), 1:162, 1:168–69.

62. Town of Boston, "The Votes and Proceedings, in Town Meeting Assembled, According to Law," 764.

63. "Four Letters on Interesting Subjects," in *American Political Writing During the Founding Era, 1760–1805*, ed. Charles S. Hyneman and Donald S. Lutz (Liberty Fund, 1983), 1:384–85.

64. Charles Inglis, "The True Interest of America Impartially Stated, in Certain Strictures on a Pamphlet Intitled Common Sense," in Wood, *The American Revolution*, 2:721.

65. Town of Essex, "Essex Result," in *The Popular Sources of Political Authority: Documents on the Massachusetts Constitution of 1780*, ed. Oscar Handlin and Mary F. Handlin (Belknap Press, 1966), 325–26, 327–32.

66. Paine, *Common Sense*, 679.

67. See John Locke, "A Letter Concerning Toleration," in *Locke on Toleration*, ed. Richard Vernon (Cambridge University Press, 2010), 30–37, especially 33. "An individual's private judgment concerning a law made for the public good on a political matter does not . . . merit toleration." The founders were misled about Locke's views on this point by William Popple's popular translation of Locke's letter, which adds to Locke's text the non-Lockean phrase "Liberty of Conscience is every mans natural Right." See John Locke, *A Letter Concerning Toleration*, trans. William Popple (Hackett, 1983), 51; Locke, "A Letter Concerning Toleration," 37; and Town of Boston, "The Votes and Proceedings, in Town Meeting Assembled, According to Law," 765. The latter erroneously cites Popple's non-Lockean introduction as part of "Lock's Letters on Toleration."

68. John Locke, *An Essay Concerning Human Understanding* (1689; Clarendon Press, 1970), 2.21.43, 2.21.47, 2.21.50–52, 2.21.59, 2.21.61.

69. See John Locke, *An Essay Concerning Human Understanding*, 2.21.55–56, 1.3.3, 1.3.13, 1.3.6: "Men in this world prefer different things, and pursue happiness by contrary courses"; the innate "desire of Happiness" operates in everyone and would "carry Men to the over-turning of all Morality" if unrestrained; and "the great variety of Opinions, concerning Moral Rules, which are to be found amongst Men, [are] according to the different sorts of Happiness, they have a Prospect of, or propose to themselves."

70. John Locke, *An Essay Concerning Human Understanding*, 2.21.45, 2.28.9.

71. See "A Defence of the Constitutions of the Government of the United States of America, Against the Attack of M. Turgot, in His Letter to Dr. Price, Dated the Twenty-Second Day of March, 1778, vol. 1," in *The Works of John Adams, Second President of the United States*, 4:466. "Americans in this age are too enlightened to be bubbled out of their liberties, even by such mighty names as Locke, Milton, Turgot, or Hume . . . they know, though Locke and Milton did not, that when popular elections are given up, liberty and free government must be given up."

72. Locke, *Two Treatises of Government*, 1.59.

73. Northwest Ordinance of 1787, art. III.

74. See Locke, *Two Treatises of Government*, 2.12: The "Laws of Countries . . . are only so far right, as they are founded on the Law of Nature, by which they are to be regulated *and interpreted*." (Emphasis added.)

75. Locke, *Two Treatises of Government*, 2.124, 2.136–37.

76. Locke, *Two Treatises of Government*, preface, 2.99.

77. Locke, *Two Treatises of Government*, 2.152, 1.168.
78. Locke, *Two Treatises of Government*, 2.95.
79. Locke, *Two Treatises of Government*, 2.107, 2.57.
80. See a similar idea from two years earlier in Thomas Jefferson, "A Summary View of the Rights of British America [1774]," in Wood, *The American Revolution*, 2:103. "When [representatives] have assumed to themselves powers which the people never put into their hands."
81. Locke, *Two Treatises of Government*, 2.135; and Hobbes, *Leviathan*, 118-20.
82. *Federalist*, no. 16 (Hamilton); "John Adams to Richard Price, 19 April 1790," in *The Works of John Adams, Second President of the United States*, 4:564.
83. *Federalist*, no. 14 (Madison).
84. Hobbes, *Leviathan*, 210; and John Locke, "A Letter Concerning Toleration," in *Locke on Toleration*, 38.
85. *Federalist*, no. 69 (Hamilton); and *Federalist*, no. 73 (Hamilton).
86. Burke, *Reflections on the Revolution in France*, 335-95.
87. "Address to the King [Jan 1777]," in *The Writings and Speeches of Edmund Burke*, 3:271; and Burke, *Reflections on the Revolution in France*, 217-21.
88. For extensive evidence of this, see Eric Nelson, *The Royalist Revolution* (Harvard University Press, 2014).
89. "Second Speech on Conciliation," in *The Writings and Speeches of Edmund Burke*, 3:195; and "Speech on Repeal of Declaratory Act," in *The Writings and Speeches of Edmund Burke*, 3:373-74.
90. "Speech on American Taxation," in *The Writings and Speeches of Edmund Burke*, 2:458; and "Letter to the Sheriffs of Bristol," in *The Writings and Speeches of Edmund Burke*, 3:313.
91. See, for instance, Otis, "The Rights of the British Colonies," 86, 111, 111-12n; "On the Tenure of the Manor of East Greenwich," in *The Papers of Benjamin Franklin, vol. 13, January 1, 1766 Through December 31, 1776*, ed. Leonard W. Labaree (Yale University Press, 1969), 22; John Dickinson, "Letters from a Farmer in Pennsylvania, to the Inhabitants of the British Colonies," in Wood, The American Revolution, 1:460; Edward Bancroft, "Remarks on the Review of the Controversy Between Great Britain and Her Colonies," in Wood, The American Revolution, 1:735-41; "To the Inhabitants of Great Britain," in *The Papers of James Iredell*, 1:263-65; James Wilson, *Considerations on the Nature and the Extent of the Legislative Authority of the British Parliament*, in Wood, *The American Revolution*, 2:145; Jefferson, "A Summary View of the Rights of British America [1774]," 2:107; and "Novanglus; or, a History of the Dispute with America, from Its Origin, in 1754, to the Present Time," in *The Works of John Adams, Second President of the United States*, 4:107-8, 114. See even the loyalist Inglis, "True Interest of America Impartially Stated, in Certain Strictures on a Pamphlet Intitled Common Sense," 761-62.
92. "Second Speech on Conciliation," in *The Writings and Speeches of Edmund Burke*, 3:193-95; and "Speech on Conway's Motion, 22 May 1776," in *The Writings and Speeches of Edmund Burke*, 3:235-36.

5

Humility, Hubris, and the Pursuit of Happiness

JANICE ROGERS BROWN

A translucent decal on the window of a muscular truck in the parking lot of a rural community center looks like a humble homage to the Constitution. Not quite. Though it begins by proclaiming, in the beautiful familiar script, "We the People," it concludes with a combative three-word coda: "have had enough."

It is a motto that could speak for a lot of Americans in our time, who have come to the view that what they want and take to be good is not what the people in charge of our civilization are after. Many Americans are not just unhappy; they are frustrated, angry, maddened, and fearful of the lumbering Leviathan that seems to control every aspect of their lives. They long ago lost their polite, fair-minded, always-for-the-underdog naivete. A sizable majority can relate to Fannie Lou Hamer's poignant riff about trying to live under the South's Jim Crow laws: "Tired," she said. "Sick and tired. . . . And sick and tired of being sick and tired."[1] They are no longer innocent. They understand how the rule of a self-righteous elite rubs the heart raw, how easily political compassion's shreds and patches allow the scarifications of contempt to show through. They increasingly have the sense that what governing elites around the world mean by happiness is nothing the American founders would deem worthy of pursuit.

William Blackstone contended that God had "so inseparably interwoven the laws of eternal justice with the happiness of each individual" that "obedience to this on one paternal precept, 'that man should pursue his own true and substantial happiness,'" is "the foundation of what we call ethics, or natural law."[2] The members of the founding generation had in mind a very specific notion of the pursuit of happiness—one that was inseparable from virtue. Their view was a unique synthesis of classical political philosophy, the Christian natural law tradition, the English common law, the republican natural rights tradition, and the insights of the commonsense philosophers of the Scottish Enlightenment. Thus, they defined happiness as the pursuit of virtue—as *being* good, rather than *feeling* good.[3]

An abundance of evidence makes clear that the American founders sought to establish a nation that relied on these essential concepts. Without their revival, the revival of our national civic project is unimaginable.

Self-Evident Truth

America is an exceptional nation. It found the sweet spot: that space equidistant from Homo sapiens and *homo deus*. Kermit the Frog used to tell us, with a wry crimp of his fabric lips, "It's not easy being green." We understood his need to flourish in his frogginess. We could have added our own baleful note to that chorus. It is not easy being human. Our deepest vulnerability is our vanity. The longest distance between two places may be time, but the longest distance between civilization and barbarity, between freedom and tyranny, between human flourishing and human failure, is hubris.

Americans were reminded from the pulpit that "liberty was an inalienable right according to the Natural Law of Creation."[4] These ideas constituted our constitutional premises. Consistent with these natural law premises, the founders "believed that certain aspects of human nature were immutable and that they tightly constrain what is politically and culturally possible."[5] The Declaration of Independence contains what philosopher Leszek Kolakowski described as "the most famous single sentence ever written in the Western Hemisphere."[6] It starts with us and ends with happiness: "We hold these truths to be self-evident, that all men are created equal, that they are endowed by their Creator with certain unalienable Rights, that among these are Life, Liberty and the pursuit of Happiness." The founders really believed that most famous statement about human beings being equal in the eyes of God and before the law. Kolakowski acknowledges that most of the writers and thinkers—ancient and modern—who have shaped the political imagination of the West reject this notion of equality.[7] And, on the eve of the nation's 250th birthday, what the founding documents meant by equality remains a hotly contested issue.

It should not be. Human equality is the plumb line of the American regime. For American statesmen of the founding era, "the fundamental nature of human beings as free and equal rights-bearers" was *the* organizing principle of politics.[8] Governments existed to secure natural rights and had to be judged by how well they secured them.

And those natural rights are the rights that ineluctably follow from the plain fact of our creation as unique individuals, each naturally striving to live and to fulfill one's innate potential. They are the rights of personal autonomy, self-improvement, self-expression, voluntary association, enjoyment of the product of one's labor, and voluntary exchange. And, as rights equal to all, they necessarily exclude any so-called "right" that advantages one person, or one class of persons, at the expense of another.

The founders exhibited a surprising degree of faith in the capacity of ordinary Americans to exercise the Declaration's principles of liberty. They incorporated that principle in the Constitution "to give the common man a voice, a veto, elbow room, a refuge from the raging presumptions of his 'betters,'" writes Thomas Sowell.[9] They recognized that no single class had a monopoly on intelligence or virtue. As Charles Murray put it, "The nobility of the American experiment lay in its allegiance to the proposition that everyone may equally aspire to happiness."[10]

Federalists and Anti-Federalists disagreed strenuously about the Constitution, arguing over the structure of government, the need for a Bill of Rights, slavery, the accountability of the judiciary, and a host of other issues. "Yet one thing still united them—the understanding that whatever form of government was to be adopted, its goal should be the happiness of the people."[11]

The founders believed the quest for happiness involved a daily practice, the daily cultivation of virtue, requiring mental and spiritual self-discipline, a lifelong endeavor to improve one's character. This stern commitment to *self*-improvement was the governing zeitgeist of America's political theology at least through the Civil War. Frederick Douglass seemed to echo the founders when he insisted virtuous habits were key to the pursuit of happiness.[12] He noted: "There can be no independence without a large share of self-dependence, and this virtue cannot be bestowed. It must be developed from within."[13]

That view of governance and its connection to happiness has largely suffused the American psyche even into the 21st century. Abraham Lincoln praised Thomas Jefferson for incorporating into the Declaration "an abstract truth, applicable to all men and all times."[14] In a 1926 speech celebrating the 150th anniversary of the Declaration, Calvin Coolidge warned that the equality of human beings and their endowment with inalienable rights was a "final" insight. Anyone who sought to deny the "truth or soundness" of that proposition would be moving "not forward, but backward toward the time when there was no equality, no rights of the individual, no rule of the people."[15]

President Coolidge ended his speech by declaring that "the things of the spirit come first" and warning that the failure to understand this aspect of the founding would cause the American project to fail.[16] This admonition was not a final rhetorical flourish. It is the key to understanding the pursuit of happiness and its connection to human flourishing.

The Denial of Truth

Rather than hold close to the Declaration's truths, however, modernity too often has followed David Hume's command at the end of his *An Enquiry Concerning Human Understanding*: If any source purports truth in matters that are not mathematical or sensory, "commit it then to the flames: for it can contain nothing but sophistry and illusion."[17]

Hume's radical empiricism has spawned a cult of quantitative method known as scientism (or reductionism), which dissolves the distinction between persons and things. Thus, man has a value no greater than "a camel or a stone or any other part of nature."[18] Yet we know, with the same "profound intuition" as the metaphysical writers and poets, like John Milton, Alexander Pope, and Jonathan Swift, that Homo sapiens must simultaneously inhabit two worlds, the physical and the metaphysical.[19] Homo sapiens—what Pope describes as "the glory, jest, and riddle of the world"—is infinitely more than merely a "part of nature."[20]

"Darwin enabled modern secular culture to heave a great collective sigh of relief, by apparently providing a way to eliminate purpose, meaning, and design as fundamental features of the world," wrote Thomas Nagel.[21] Actually, as Edward Feser observes, the idea that science eliminates purpose, meaning, and design predates Charles Darwin by several hundred years and may owe more to modern secularist philosophers like Thomas Hobbes and Hume and anti-medieval philosophers like René Descartes, Immanuel Kant, and John Locke than to science.

To acknowledge that the origin of life is a mystery might unseat materialism as the religion of our time. It is only when materialistic assumptions are taken for granted and the classical alternative is neglected that philosophical arguments for the traditional religious worldview (e.g., for the existence of God and the natural law conception of morality) can be made to seem problematic.[22] As G. K. Chesterton described the fatal sequence, we have been victimized by the "disputed system of thought which began with Evolution and ... ended in Eugenics."[23]

Just as many religious, philosophical, and intellectual streams converged to bring about the moment when the American regime could come into being, many pseudo religions, philosophical errors, scientific superstitions, and just-so stories converged to threaten its dissolution. Darwinism facilitated the rise of scientific materialism, and happily for the progressives, it jibed with their desire to make man's mind man's fate. Scientific materialism was the God of the progressive age.

Dethroning the "Great I Am" of divine sovereignty sets the stage for the abolition of man. Not only is there no self-evident truth; there is no truth at all. Subjection to "the grand sez who?" of moral relativism not only means that there can be no normative grounding for any ethical system; it means there can be no rule of law, no truth, and no freedom. As C. S. Lewis explained, "A dogmatic belief in objective value is necessary to the very idea of a rule which is not tyranny or an obedience which is not slavery."[24]

The sovereign myth in the old dark age was that "everything means everything."[25] The sovereign myth in our more enlightened times is that "nothing means anything."[26] It took the "anointed"—the self-righteous elite whose cosmic vision compels them to lord over the rest of humanity—roughly 200 years to pollute the wellspring of all the religious, philosophical, and intellectual streams that converged to bring about the American project. They subtracted God from the equation, and with God missing, the right to actualize one's unique God-given purpose through self-improvement and hard work devolved into a right to indulge appetites and material desires. With God missing, a government that had existed to guarantee freedom devolved into a government that existed to guarantee free stuff.

Perhaps the foremost modern proponent of nothingness is Yuval Noah Harari. Harari is an Israeli historian whose penchant for big history has produced a couple of bestsellers. His first book, *Sapiens*, is a sprawling narrative of the whole history of earth, containing—as John Sexton relates—little "actual history," much "speculative reconstruction of human evolution," and some bold prognostications about the future of humankind.[27] Harari seems oblivious to the fact that he is participating in a debate that has "raged for centuries between those who assert the primacy of metaphysical knowledge and those who argue for the priority of physical reality."[28] The powerful appeal of the material world's exclusive claim to reality is born, Lewis suggested, of the hatred of death, the fear of true immortality, and the hope for a man-created eternal life—what Lewis called "the sweet poison of the false infinite."[29]

According to Harari, humans are an animal of no consequence that would have remained a "middle-of-the-road, middle-of-the-food-chain species"[30] had we not started making things up—imagining things like gods, laws, rights, ethical principles, and limited liability corporations. Harari insists that science, particularly biology, is the answer to every question and precludes any hint of transcendence. Thus, there are no gods, no human rights, no souls, no laws beyond the common imagination of human beings, and no universal and immutable principles such as equality or justice. These imagined realities may be "vital, significant, and world changing," but they are not real.[31]

Happiness as Narcotic

Back in the fabled year 1989 (when history was said to have ended), Australian philosopher David Stove wrote a book that began with Homer's observation that "humans are the unhappiest of all creatures."[32] Stove identified the "enlarged benevolence" of the English Enlightenment as a significant source of modern discontent.[33] The main teachings of this particular branch of the Enlightenment were secularism, egalitarianism, and the utilitarian axiom that the test of morality is the greatest happiness of the greatest number. Thus, beginning in the 18th century, benevolence became the highest virtue, eclipsing both the monastic virtues—humility, chastity, and obedience—and the warrior virtues—courage, loyalty, patriotism, and justice. The conception of happiness was thus dramatically changed.

While the Stoics and "moral sense" philosophers saw the pursuit of happiness as a quest rather than a destination, a practice including responsibilities as well as rights (and especially the responsibility to limit, master, and restrain selfish instincts), proto-utilitarians met their quota of virtue through benevolence—even if they did so with other people's property. And there was an irresistible bonus. They could applaud their own magnanimity as they promoted the happiness of the beneficiaries of their largesse. Happiness in this context was not about character, self-improvement, or sustained effort. It was all about stuff—*free* stuff, if you could get it.

Stove and Robert Nozick propose similar thought experiments. Suppose, Stove says, medical technology advances to the point that

> the way for a human being to be happiest is to be kept permanently in a hospital bottle, with the brain suitably stimulated by chemical or electrical means. All the pleasures of normal life, and none of the pains, might be experienced in this way, even though the "life" being led is entirely hallucinatory.[34]

Nozick likewise invited readers to suppose the existence of "an experience machine that would give you any experience you desired."[35] "Super-duper neuropsychologists could stimulate your brain so that you would think and feel you were writing a great novel" (or reading one), transforming you into whatever sort of person you would like to be. Would plugging into such a machine be a kind of suicide, or would it limit us to a man-made reality when we would prefer to be open to a deeper significance? Whether we have an experience machine, a transformation machine, or a result machine, Nozick suggests that "perhaps what we desire is to live (an active verb) ourselves, in contact with reality."[36] And the answers, if we can find them, will relate to free will and the nature of consciousness.

Stove's and Nozick's thought experiments anticipated the iconic 1999 movie *The Matrix*. In that film, it is 2199, and in an AI push gone awry, the machines have conquered humanity. The only use the machines have for humankind is as a sort of bio-battery. To keep the fuel cells operating optimally, they let people live full lives, complete with work, challenges, and triumphs, all virtual. Human beings have no choice about what they think or dream. But they are happy, in a way.

It is hard to escape the sense that this is what a lot of Western elites have in mind for their fellow citizens. Of course, our captivity won't be as sophisticated as the matrix, and our pleasures not quite so seamless, but with pharmacological mood enhancement and dazzling digital entertainment, we will never guess that life could be different, or better, or *real*—and, of course, we would be sure to vote as we have been told to vote, imagining that we live in a free democracy.

According to Harari's version of the life sciences, "Happiness and suffering are nothing but different balances of bodily sensations."[37] "People," he says, "are made happy by one thing and one thing only—pleasant sensations in their bodies."[38] And as Sexton relates, Harari claims that—despite the abundance of our creature comforts—we modern people are no happier than premodern people. But Sexton also points out that Harari does not reach this conclusion by contrasting the modern way of life with the classical understanding of happiness as a state achieved by those who live good lives in accord with their nature. Instead, Harari relies on opinion surveys and the findings of the new science of happiness.[39]

A total eclipse of the human person is central to Harari's thesis. But without an endgame, his arguments seem not only inchoate but incoherent. Even Harari admits the comforting illusions he so blithely dismisses are necessary to allow liberal democratic societies to flourish. But as Harari explains in *Homo Deus*, the lack of rights will not matter, since humanity reimagined and reengineered will be upgraded into gods—albeit gods without goodness, without grace, without purity, possessed of superhuman bodily and mental faculties but far from the God Who is the alpha and omega; Who was, is, and always will be; Who created the cosmos and has a plan for the world and a purpose for mankind. No. "At the end of the theological road laid out by would-be priests" like Harari, "there is no more American civilization, Western civilization, or human civilization."[40]

Putting Transcendence Back into the Equation

In his last essay, Lewis declared, "We have no right to happiness." He was not, as Justin Dyer explains, taking issue with the American founders. The Declaration of Independence posited that "all men had an equal right to pursue happiness within the bounds of the moral law."[41] Thus, natural law confers the right to *pursue* happiness, not the right to have it unearned. The moral philosophy of the founding affirmed "that natural law has a lawgiver," a creator separate and distinct from creation, and that creator imbued his creation with reason capable of grasping "moral goods that are real rather than nominal or subjective."[42] Natural law can never be interpreted to confer the "moral right simply to take what we want to satisfy our desires, whatever those desires happen to be."[43] The old idea that might makes right, that the strong do what they will and the weak endure, was precisely what the revolutionary generation repudiated.

The result has been a profound misunderstanding of the pursuit of happiness. Instead of a spiritual quest for self-expression, self-perfection, and self-mastery, the pursuit of happiness has been transformed into a justification for the permissive cornucopia of the welfare state and rhetorical support for every conceivable hedonistic excess.

The founders pursued happiness in a way that modeled the self-restraint necessary for true freedom. Only a community of people capable of self-discipline is fit for self-government. To the founders, freedom was never a license for mere indulgence. Liberty could never be allowed to tip into licentiousness. Rather, the founding generation articulated and accepted moral boundaries, and the community had a right, indeed an obligation, to curb destructive conduct. As John Adams wrote, "Our Constitution was made only for a moral and religious People. It is wholly inadequate to the government of any other."[44] For the founders, true happiness was achieved in rational creativity, not in the satiation of passionate desire; happiness was eudaemonic, not hedonic.

The American Revolution and the French Revolution are sometimes described as comparable. Although they seem to be products of the same historical moment, they actually lie on opposite sides of a great divide. Jacques Barzun divides modern history—the past 500 years—this way: The years 1500–1660 were dominated by the issue of what to believe regarding God and religion, the years 1661–1789 by what to do about the status of the individual and the mode of government, and the years

1790–1920 by the question of how social and economic equality should be achieved.[45] The American Revolution is on one side of the latter great divide; the French Revolution is on the other. The American Revolution represented the culmination of religious consciousness applied to the design of government; the French Revolution heralded the beginning of the secular age. And this profound discontinuity in worldview has made all the difference.

The human longing to be free derives, perhaps, from a simple incantation: "Let there be light."[46] This is the essence of the *imago dei*, the reason God is mindful of man who ranks, the apostle reminds us, only "a little lower than the angels."[47] Michelangelo famously painted this scene—*The Creation of Adam*—on the ceiling of the Sistine Chapel. A recumbent deity stretches out a single finger toward a new creature. The artist depicts a quiet moment. This is not the God of thunder and lightning, volcanoes and tumult, and yet it seems that all creation awaits what will pass between them. A divine spark. What if God's utterance was calling forth not just the creative properties of light but consciousness itself? Paul Davies expresses wonder that Homo sapiens carries the spark of rationality that unlocks the universe. Remarkably, "we, who are the children of the universe—animated stardust—can . . . reflect on the nature of that same universe, even to the extent of glimpsing the rules on which it runs."[48] What if consciousness, not matter, is the ultimate foundation of the universe?

This idea seems at least as plausible as the multiverse. Despite the mutterings of the acolytes of scientism that the material world is all that exists,

> the five cardinal mysteries of the nonmaterial mind remain unaccounted for: subjective awareness, free will, how memories are stored, the "higher" faculties of reason and imagination, and that unique sense of personal identity that changes and matures over time but remains resolutely the same.[49]

As a youngster, George Washington laboriously copied a list of "Rules of Civility and Decent Behavior" that he had found in a book. Most of the rules concerned manners and deportment, but the last rule reads, "Labour to keep alive in your Breast that Little Spark of Celestial fire Called Conscience."[50] That definition of conscience—the "little spark of celestial fire"—still has resonance today. If you believe, as seems likely, that by a "little spark of celestial fire," he meant a moral compass, an understanding of man's limitations, and an innate sense of right and wrong, then it is that "little spark" that led Washington and others to establish a constitutional government based on equality under law, unalienable rights, and government by consent.

According to Barzun's historical survey, which ends in 1920, scientists and philosophers spent roughly three centuries trying to organize society as if God did not exist and roughly two centuries seeking to reshape society through industrial development, social engineering, and various systems of wealth creation and redistribution. This process was supposed to bring forth the new man, an improved version of humanity. The 20th century was the culmination of that process. But alas, the new man failed to arrive.

If we were to extend Barzun's survey of modern history to the present, we would have to describe 1920 to 2025 as the period in which the attempt to abolish man, not to improve him, became the avowed goal of the ruling class in Western democracies. The earlier claim that malleable human nature could be reengineered to bring about the longed-for utopia has been abandoned. Lincoln warned long ago that the thirst of some men for power and distinction would be satisfied one way or another, whether by freeing the enslaved or by enslaving the free.[51] But in the 21st century, even power and distinction are not enough. The light of God must also be eclipsed. The hubris of the so-called scholars and intellectuals of today's socialist democratic regimes ensured that a world once filled with God's glory and governed by natural law became a world suffused with matter and governed by positive law. Thus, the coercive utopias of authoritarian regimes and the permissive cornucopias of socialist democracies are revealed to be evil twins. The dark impulse of despotism and the demon in democracy are identical.

The solution to our global era of crisis is not paternalistic domination. Rather, it is something higher, deeper, greater. We already know what it is. As Samuel Johnson noted, "Men more frequently require to be reminded than informed."[52] The real effect of secularism, and her handmaiden scientism, is to limit our imagination.

But contra Harari, our imagination remains more real than the flattened landscape of scientism. We bask in the starlight and thrive in the sun because the regularity and renewal of cosmic wonder conjures a metaphysical reality so vivid, awesome, and marvelous that reverence is the only rational response. The consensus gentium, the common sense of mankind, is the antidote to the corrosive skepticism of fastidious elites that could destroy the foundations of the moral order. "Man is man because he can recognize supernatural realities, not because he can invent them."[53] Michael E. Aeschliman declares that *sapienta* is an exalted form of common sense.[54] And this "integrative metaphysical-ethical vision is the irreducible, indispensable prerogative, privilege, and patrimony of human civilization itself" and a necessary prerequisite of any vision of true human happiness.[55]

More importantly, the recovery and restoration of what we already know may not take centuries—though certainly it will be a generational task. We must revive our faith in God's providence and creative power and in the central role that God assigned humanity. We must regain a proper sense of humility and recommit ourselves to the self-mastery, candor, fortitude, and selflessness requisite to self-government.

Notes

1. Maegan Parker Brooks and Davis W. Houck, eds., *The Speeches of Fannie Lou Hamer: To Tell It Like It Is* (University Press of Mississippi, 2013), 62.

2. William Blackstone, *Commentaries on the Laws of England*, vol. 1, 1765–1769 (Clarendon Press, 1765), 40–41.

3. Jeffrey Rosen, *The Pursuit of Happiness: How Classical Writers on Virtue Inspired the Lives of the Founders and Defined America* (Simon & Schuster, 2024), 6.

4. Rod Gragg, *Forged in Faith: How Faith Shaped the Birth of the Nation 1607–1776* (Howard Books, 2010), 156.

5. Charles Murray, *Coming Apart: The State of White America, 1960–2010* (Forum Books, 2012), 301.

6. Leszek Kolakowski, "The Idolatry of Politics," lecture, 15th Annual Jefferson Lecture, National Endowment for the Humanities, Washington, DC, May 7, 1986.

7. Kolakowski, "The Idolatry of Politics."

8. James R. Zink, "The Language of Law and Liberty," *The American Political Science Review* 103, no. 3 (2009): 442–43, https://www.cambridge.org/core/journals/american-political-science-review/article/abs/language-of-liberty-and-law-james-wilson-on-americas-written-constitution/BDBA747B5508658594FB2CA482C7D7F8.

9. Thomas Sowell, *The Quest for Cosmic Justice* (Free Press, 1999), 146.

10. Charles Murray, *In Pursuit: Of Happiness and Good Government* (1988; Liberty Fund, 2013), 141.

11. Ryan Rynbrandt, "The Pursuit of Happiness," paper presented at the Western Political Science Association 2016 Annual Conference, San Diego, CA, March 25, 2016, https://www.wpsanet.org/papers/docs/rynbrandt.pdf.

12. Rynbrandt, *The Pursuit of Happiness*, 246.

13. Frederick Douglass, "Self-Made Men," speech, Carlisle, PA, March 1893, 15, https://www.loc.gov/resource/mss11879.29002/.

14. Abraham Lincoln to Henry L. Pierce and Others, April 6, 1859, https://teachingamericanhistory.org/document/letter-to-henry-pierce-and-others/.

15. Calvin Coolidge, "The Inspiration of the Declaration," speech, Philadelphia, PA, July 5, 1926, https://coolidgefoundation.org/resources/inspiration-of-the-declaration-of-independence/.

16. Coolidge, "The Inspiration of the Declaration."

17. David Hume, *An Enquiry Concerning Human Understanding* (London, 1748), sec. 12, pt. 3, 132.

18. David Hume, *An Enquiry Concerning Human Understanding*, 84.

19. Michael E. Aeschliman, *The Restoration of Man: C. S. Lewis and the Continuing Case Against Scientism* (Discovery Institute Press, 2019), 50–53.

20. Jacob Bronowski, *The Identity of Man* (Natural History Press, 1965), 2.

21. Thomas Nagel, *The Last Word* (Oxford University Press, 2001), 131.

22. Edward Feser, *The Last Superstition: A Refutation of the New Atheism* (St. Augustine Press, 2008), 13.

23. G. K. Chesterton, *Eugenics and Other Evils* (Cassell and Company, 1922), 77.

24. C. S. Lewis, *The Abolition of Man* (Macmillan, 1947), 84–85.

25. Thomas Howard, *Chance or the Dance? A Critique of Modern Secularism* (Ignatius Press, 2018), 134.

26. Howard, *Chance or the Dance?*

27. John Sexton, "A Reductionist History of Humankind," *The New Atlantis*, Fall 2015, 110, https://www.thenewatlantis.com/publications/a-reductionist-history-of-humankind.

28. Aeschliman, *The Restoration of Man*, 45.

29. C. S. Lewis, *Perelandra* (Simon & Schuster, 1996), 81–82.

30. Nick Spencer, "Sapiens, Maybe; Deus, No: The Problem with Yuval Noah Harari," ABC Australia, July 13, 2020, https://www.abc.net.au/religion/the-problem-with-yuval-noah-harari/12451764.

31. Spencer, "Sapiens, Maybe; Deus, No."

32. Homer, *The Odyssey*, bk. 18, lines 130–37.

33. David Stove, *What's Wrong with Benevolence: Happiness, Private Property, and the Limits of Enlightenment* (Encounter Books, 2011).

34. Stove, *What's Wrong with Benevolence*, 98.

35. Robert Nozick, *Anarchy, State, and Utopia* (Basic Books, 1977), 42–44.

36. Nozick, *Anarchy, State, and Utopia*, 45.

37. Yuval Noah Harari, *Homo Deus: A Brief History of Tomorrow* (Harvill Secker, 2016).

38. Yuval Noah Harari, *Sapiens: A Brief Human History of Mankind* (Harper, 2015).

39. Sexton, "A Reductionist History of Humankind."

40. James Poulos, "Big Tech: Sacred Culture or Cyborg Rapture," in *Against the Great Reset: Eighteen Theses Contra the New World Order*, ed. Michael Walsh (Bombardier Books, 2022), 138.

41. Justin Dyer, "The God of the Declaration," James Wilson Institute, Anchoring Truths, July 4, 2022, https://www.anchoringtruths.org/the-god-of-the-declaration/.

42. Dyer, "The God of the Declaration."

43. Dyer, "The God of the Declaration."

44. John Adams to the Massachusetts Militia, October 11, 1798, Founders Online, https://founders.archives.gov/documents/Adams/99-02-02-3102.

45. Jacques Barzun, *From Dawn to Decadence: 500 Years of Western Cultural Life, 1500 to the Present* (HarperCollins, 2000), xvii.

46. Gen. 1:3 (NIV).

47. Heb. 2:7; and Ps. 8:5 (NIV).

48. Paul Davies, *The Mind of God: The Scientific Basis for a Rational World* (Simon & Schuster, 1992), 232.

49. James Le Fanu, "Foreword," in *The Restoration of Man*.

50. George Washington, "The Rules of Civility," George Washington's Mount Vernon, https://www.mountvernon.org/george-washington/rules-of-civility?page=10.

51. Abraham Lincoln, "Speech Before the Young Men's Lyceum of Springfield, Illinois," speech, Springfield, IL, January 27, 1838, in John Gabriel Hunt, *The Essential Abraham Lincoln* (Gramercy, 1993), 8, 15.

52. Samuel Johnson, "No. 2: The Necessity and Danger of Looking into Futurity," *The Rambler*, March 24, 1750.

53. C. S. Lewis, *The Allegory of Love* (Oxford University Press, 1958), 158–59.
54. Aeschliman, *The Restoration of Man*, 66.
55. Aeschliman, *The Restoration of Man*, 124.

About the Authors

Janice Rogers Brown is a lecturer and senior fellow at the public law and policy program at the University of California, Berkeley, School of Law. She was a judge on the US Court of Appeals for the DC Circuit and on the California Supreme Court.

Daniel E. Burns is an associate professor of politics at the University of Dallas and a visiting fellow at the Civitas Institute at the University of Texas at Austin.

Robert P. George is a nonresident senior fellow at the American Enterprise Institute and the McCormick Professor of Jurisprudence and director of the James Madison Program in American Ideals and Institutions at Princeton University.

Charles R. Kesler is the Dengler-Dykema Distinguished Professor of Government at Claremont McKenna College and the editor of the *Claremont Review of Books*.

Michael Zuckert is the Nancy Reeves Dreux Professor Emeritus of Political Science at the University of Notre Dame and clinical professor at Arizona State University.

About the Editors

Yuval Levin is the director of Social, Cultural, and Constitutional Studies at the American Enterprise Institute, where he also holds the Beth and Ravenel Curry Chair in Public Policy. The founder and editor of *National Affairs*, he is also a senior editor at *The New Atlantis*, a contributing editor at *National Review*, and a contributing opinion writer at *The New York Times*.

Adam J. White is the Laurence H. Silberman Chair in Constitutional Governance and a senior fellow at the American Enterprise Institute, where he focuses on the Supreme Court and the administrative state. Concurrently, he codirects the Antonin Scalia Law School's C. Boyden Gray Center for the Study of the Administrative State.

John Yoo is a nonresident senior fellow at the American Enterprise Institute; the Emanuel S. Heller Professor of Law at the University of California, Berkeley; and a visiting fellow at the Hoover Institution.

The American Enterprise Institute for Public Policy Research

AEI is a nonpartisan, nonprofit research and educational organization. The work of our scholars and staff advances ideas rooted in our commitment to expanding individual liberty, increasing opportunity, and strengthening freedom.

The Institute engages in research; publishes books, papers, studies, and short-form commentary; and conducts seminars and conferences. AEI's research activities are carried out under four major departments: Domestic Policy Studies, Economic Policy Studies, Foreign and Defense Policy Studies, and Social, Cultural, and Constitutional Studies. The resident scholars and fellows listed in these pages are part of a network that also includes nonresident scholars at top universities.

The views expressed in AEI publications are those of the authors; AEI does not take institutional positions on any issues.

BOARD OF TRUSTEES

DANIEL A. D'ANIELLO, *Chairman*
Cofounder and Chairman Emeritus
The Carlyle Group

CLIFFORD S. ASNESS
Managing and Founding Principal
AQR Capital Management LLC

PETER H. COORS
Chairman of the Board
Molson Coors Brewing Company

HARLAN CROW
Chairman
Crow Holdings

RAVENEL B. CURRY III
Chief Investment Officer
Eagle Capital Management LLC

KIMBERLY O. DENNIS
President and CEO
Searle Freedom Trust

DICK DEVOS
President
The Windquest Group

ROBERT DOAR
President
American Enterprise Institute

BEHDAD EGHBALI
Managing Partner and Cofounder
Clearlake Capital Group LP

MARTIN C. ELTRICH III
Partner
AEA Investors LP

TULLY M. FRIEDMAN
Managing Director, Retired
FFL Partners LLC

CHRISTOPHER B. GALVIN
Chairman
Harrison Street Capital LLC

HARVEY GOLUB
Chairman and CEO, Retired,
 American Express Company
Chairman, Miller Buckfire

FRANK J. HANNA
CEO
Hanna Capital LLC

BILL HASLAM
Former Governor of Tennessee

DEEPA JAVERI
Chief Financial Officer
XRHealth

JOANNA F. JONSSON
Vice Chair, Capital Group
President, Capital Research
 Management Company

MARC S. LIPSCHULTZ
Co-CEO
Blue Owl Capital

JOHN A. LUKE JR.
Chairman
WestRock Company

DREW MCKNIGHT
Co-CEO and Managing Partner
Fortress Investment Group

BOB MURLEY
Senior Adviser
UBS

PAT NEAL
Chairman of the Executive Committee
Neal Communities

ROSS PEROT JR.
Chairman
Hillwood Development Company

GEOFFREY S. REHNERT
Co-CEO
Audax Group

MATTHEW K. ROSE
Retired CEO and Chairman
BNSF Railway

EDWARD B. RUST JR.
Chairman Emeritus
State Farm Insurance Companies

WILSON H. TAYLOR
Chairman Emeritus
Cigna Corporation

WILLIAM H. WALTON
Managing Member
Rockpoint Group LLC

WILL WEATHERFORD
Managing Partner
Weatherford Capital

EMERITUS TRUSTEES

THE HONORABLE
RICHARD B. CHENEY

JOHN FARACI

ROBERT F. GREENHILL

BRUCE KOVNER

KEVIN B. ROLLINS

D. GIDEON SEARLE

OFFICERS

ROBERT DOAR
President

JASON BERTSCH
Executive Vice President

KAZUKI KO
Senior Vice President;
Chief Financial Officer

KATHERYNE WALKER
Senior Vice President of Operations;
Chief Human Resources Officer

MATTHEW CONTINETTI
Senior Fellow; Director, Domestic
Policy Studies; Patrick and Charlene
Neal Chair in American Prosperity

YUVAL LEVIN
Senior Fellow; Director, Social,
Cultural, and Constitutional Studies;
Beth and Ravenel Curry Chair in Public
Policy; Editor in Chief, National Affairs

KORI SCHAKE
Senior Fellow; Director, Foreign and
Defense Policy Studies

MICHAEL R. STRAIN
Senior Fellow; Director, Economic
Policy Studies; Arthur F. Burns Scholar
in Political Economy

RESEARCH STAFF

SAMUEL J. ABRAMS
Nonresident Senior Fellow

BETH AKERS
Senior Fellow

J. JOEL ALICEA
Nonresident Fellow

JOSEPH ANTOS
Senior Fellow Emeritus

LEON ARON
Senior Fellow

KIRSTEN AXELSEN
Nonresident Fellow

JOHN BAILEY
Nonresident Senior Fellow

KYLE BALZER
Jeane Kirkpatrick Fellow

CLAUDE BARFIELD
Senior Fellow

MICHAEL BARONE
Senior Fellow Emeritus

MICHAEL BECKLEY
Nonresident Senior Fellow

ERIC J. BELASCO
Nonresident Senior Fellow

ANDREW G. BIGGS
Senior Fellow

MASON M. BISHOP
Nonresident Fellow

DAN BLUMENTHAL
Senior Fellow

KARLYN BOWMAN
Distinguished Senior Fellow Emeritus

HAL BRANDS
Senior Fellow

ALEX BRILL
Senior Fellow

ARTHUR C. BROOKS
President Emeritus

DANIEL BUCK
Research Fellow

RICHARD BURKHAUSER
Nonresident Senior Fellow

CLAY CALVERT
Nonresident Senior Fellow

JAMES C. CAPRETTA
Senior Fellow; Milton Friedman Chair

TIMOTHY P. CARNEY
Senior Fellow

AMITABH CHANDRA
Nonresident Senior Fellow

LYNNE V. CHENEY
Distinguished Senior Fellow

YVONNE CHIU
Jeane Kirkpatrick Fellow

JAMES W. COLEMAN
Nonresident Senior Fellow

HEATHER A. CONLEY
Nonresident Fellow

PRESTON COOPER
Senior Fellow

ZACK COOPER
Senior Fellow

KEVIN CORINTH
Senior Fellow; Deputy Director, Center on Opportunity and Social Mobility

JAY COST
Gerald R. Ford Nonresident Senior Fellow

DANIEL A. COX
Senior Fellow; Director, Survey Center on American Life

SADANAND DHUME
Senior Fellow

GISELLE DONNELLY
Senior Fellow

ROSS DOUTHAT
Nonresident Fellow

LAURA DOVE
Nonresident Fellow

COLIN DUECK
Nonresident Senior Fellow

MACKENZIE EAGLEN
Senior Fellow

NICHOLAS EBERSTADT
Henry Wendt Chair in Political Economy

JEFFREY EISENACH
Nonresident Senior Fellow

CHRISTINE EMBA
Senior Fellow

ANDREW FERGUSON
Nonresident Fellow

JESÚS FERNÁNDEZ-VILLAVERDE
John H. Makin Visiting Scholar

JOHN G. FERRARI
Nonresident Senior Fellow

JOHN C. FORTIER
Senior Fellow

ANEMONE FRANZ
Visiting Research Fellow

AARON FRIEDBERG
Nonresident Senior Fellow

JOSEPH B. FULLER
Nonresident Senior Fellow

ARTHUR GAILES
Research Fellow

SCOTT GANZ
Nonresident Fellow

R. RICHARD GEDDES
Nonresident Senior Fellow

ROBERT P. GEORGE
Nonresident Senior Fellow

EDWARD L. GLAESER
Nonresident Senior Fellow

JOSEPH W. GLAUBER
Nonresident Senior Fellow

JONAH GOLDBERG
Senior Fellow; Asness Chair in Applied Liberty

SAMUEL GOLDMAN
Visiting Fellow

JACK LANDMAN GOLDSMITH
Nonresident Senior Fellow

BARRY K. GOODWIN
Nonresident Senior Fellow

SCOTT GOTTLIEB, MD
Senior Fellow

PHIL GRAMM
Nonresident Senior Fellow

WILLIAM C. GREENWALT
Senior Fellow

ALLEN GUELZO
Nonresident Senior Fellow

PHILIP HAMBURGER
Nonresident Senior Fellow

JIM HARPER
Nonresident Senior Fellow

TODD HARRISON
Senior Fellow

WILLIAM HAUN
Nonresident Fellow

FREDERICK M. HESS
Senior Fellow; Director, Education Policy Studies

CAROLE HOOVEN
Nonresident Senior Fellow

BRONWYN HOWELL
Nonresident Senior Fellow

R. GLENN HUBBARD
Nonresident Senior Fellow

HOWARD HUSOCK
Senior Fellow

BENEDIC N. IPPOLITO
Senior Fellow

MARK JAMISON
Nonresident Senior Fellow

FREDERICK W. KAGAN
Senior Fellow; Director, Critical Threats Project

STEVEN B. KAMIN
Senior Fellow

LEON R. KASS, MD
Senior Fellow Emeritus

JOSHUA T. KATZ
Senior Fellow

L. LYNNE KIESLING
Nonresident Senior Fellow

KLON KITCHEN
Nonresident Senior Fellow

KEVIN R. KOSAR
Senior Fellow

PAUL H. KUPIEC
Senior Fellow

DESMOND LACHMAN
Senior Fellow

PAUL LETTOW
Senior Fellow

DANIEL LYONS
Nonresident Senior Fellow

NAT MALKUS
Senior Fellow; Deputy Director, Education Policy Studies

JOHN D. MAURER
Nonresident Fellow

ELAINE MCCUSKER
Senior Fellow

BRUCE D. MEYER
Nonresident Senior Fellow

BRIAN J. MILLER
Nonresident Fellow

CHRIS MILLER
Nonresident Senior Fellow

THOMAS P. MILLER
Senior Fellow

M. ANTHONY MILLS
Senior Fellow; Director, Center for Technology, Science, and Energy

FERDINANDO MONTE
Nonresident Senior Fellow

CHARLES MURRAY
F. A. Hayek Chair Emeritus in Cultural Studies

STEPHEN D. OLINER
Senior Fellow Emeritus

BRENT ORRELL
Senior Fellow

TOBIAS PETER
Senior Fellow; Codirector, AEI Housing Center

JAMES PETHOKOUKIS
Senior Fellow; Editor, AEIdeas Blog; DeWitt Wallace Chair

ROGER PIELKE JR.
Senior Fellow

EDWARD J. PINTO
Senior Fellow; Codirector, AEI Housing Center

DANIELLE PLETKA
Distinguished Senior Fellow

KYLE POMERLEAU
Senior Fellow

ROBERT PONDISCIO
Senior Fellow

RAMESH PONNURU
Nonresident Senior Fellow

ROB PORTMAN
Distinguished Visiting Fellow in the Practice of Public Policy

ANGELA RACHIDI
Senior Fellow; Rowe Scholar

NAOMI SCHAEFER RILEY
Senior Fellow

WILL RINEHART
Senior Fellow

DALIBOR ROHAC
Senior Fellow

CHRISTINE ROSEN
Senior Fellow

JEFFREY A. ROSEN
Nonresident Fellow

MICHAEL M. ROSEN
Nonresident Senior Fellow

IAN ROWE
Senior Fellow

MICHAEL RUBIN
Senior Fellow

PAUL RYAN
Distinguished Visiting Fellow in the Practice of Public Policy

DANIEL SAMET
Jeane Kirkpatrick Fellow

SALLY SATEL, MD
Senior Fellow

ERIC SAYERS
Nonresident Fellow

CHRISTOPHER J. SCALIA
Senior Fellow

BRETT D. SCHAEFER
Senior Fellow

DIANA SCHAUB
Nonresident Senior Fellow

ANNA SCHERBINA
Nonresident Senior Fellow

GARY J. SCHMITT
Senior Fellow

MARK SCHNEIDER
Nonresident Senior Fellow

DEREK SCISSORS
Senior Fellow

DAVID SHAYWITZ
Adjunct Fellow

NEENA SHENAI
Nonresident Fellow

DAN SLATER
Nonresident Fellow

SITA NATARAJ SLAVOV
Nonresident Senior Fellow

THOMAS SMITH
Nonresident Fellow

VINCENT H. SMITH
Nonresident Senior Fellow

CHRISTINA HOFF SOMMERS
Senior Fellow Emeritus

DANIEL STID
Nonresident Senior Fellow

CHRIS STIREWALT
Senior Fellow

BENJAMIN STOREY
Senior Fellow

JENNA SILBER STOREY
Senior Fellow

RUY TEIXEIRA
Nonresident Senior Fellow

SHANE TEWS
Nonresident Senior Fellow

MARC A. THIESSEN
Senior Fellow

JOSEPH S. TRACY
Nonresident Senior Fellow

SEAN TRENDE
Nonresident Fellow

TUNKU VARADARAJAN
Nonresident Fellow

STAN VEUGER
Senior Fellow

ALAN D. VIARD
Senior Fellow Emeritus

DUSTIN WALKER
Nonresident Fellow

PHILIP WALLACH
Senior Fellow

PETER J. WALLISON
Senior Fellow Emeritus

MARK J. WARSHAWSKY
Senior Fellow; Wilson H. Taylor Chair in Health Care and Retirement Policy

MATT WEIDINGER
Senior Fellow; Rowe Scholar

ADAM J. WHITE
Senior Fellow; Laurence H. Silberman Chair in Constitutional Governance

BRAD WILCOX
Nonresident Senior Fellow

THOMAS CHATTERTON WILLIAMS
Nonresident Fellow

SCOTT WINSHIP
Senior Fellow; Director, Center on Opportunity and Social Mobility

AUDRYE WONG
Jeane Kirkpatrick Fellow

JOHN YOO
Nonresident Senior Fellow

BENJAMIN ZYCHER
Senior Fellow

www.ingramcontent.com/pod-product-compliance
Lightning Source LLC
Jackson TN
JSHW071107090925
90732JS00005B/16